"Family means putting your arms around each other and being there."

—Barbara Bush

SECRETS from GRANDMA'S ATTIC

History Lost and Found
The Art of Deception
Testament to a Patriot
Buttoned Up
Pearl of Great Price
Hidden Riches
Movers and Shakers
The Eye of the Cat
Refined by Fire
The Prince and the Popper
Something Shady
Duel Threat
A Royal Tea
The Heart of a Hero
Fractured Beauty
A Shadowy Past
In Its Time
Nothing Gold Can Stay
The Cameo Clue
Veiled Intentions
Turn Back the Dial
A Marathon of Kindness
A Thief in the Night

SECRETS From GRANDMA'S ATTIC

A Thief in the Night

Beth Adams

Published by Guideposts
100 Reserve Road, Suite E200
Danbury, CT 06810
Guideposts.org

Copyright © 2024 by Guideposts. All rights reserved.

This book, or parts thereof, may not be reproduced, stored in a retrieval system, or transmitted in any form or by any means, electronic, mechanical, photocopying, recording, or otherwise, without the written permission of the publisher.

This is a work of fiction. While the setting of Secrets from Grandma's Attic as presented in this series is fictional, the location of Canton, Missouri, actually exists, and some places and characters may be based on actual places and people whose identities have been used with permission or fictionalized to protect their privacy. Apart from the actual people, events, and locales that figure into the fiction narrative, all other names, characters, businesses, and events are the creation of the author's imagination and any resemblance to actual persons or events is coincidental.

Every attempt has been made to credit the sources of copyrighted material used in this book. If any such acknowledgment has been inadvertently omitted or miscredited, receipt of such information would be appreciated.

Scripture references are from the following sources: *The Holy Bible, King James Version* (KJV). *The Holy Bible, New International Version* (NIV). Copyright © 1973, 1978, 1984, 2011 by Biblica, Inc. Used by permission of Zondervan. All rights reserved worldwide. www.zondervan.com

Cover and interior design by Müllerhaus
Cover illustration by Greg Copeland at Illustration Online LLC.
Typeset by Aptara, Inc.

ISBN 978-1-961126-44-2 (hardcover)
ISBN 978-1-961126-45-9 (epub)

Printed and bound in the United States of America
10 9 8 7 6 5 4 3 2

A Thief in the Night

Chapter One

Tracy Doyle and her husband, Jeff, stood on the porch and waved goodbye as the last of their guests trickled from their home. Tracy's cousin Tom and his wife, Angie—who were visiting Canton—pulled away from the curb, and Robert West, a retired ferryboat captain and longtime fixture in town, slowly made his way to his car. Bethany Hill, a young reporter at the newspaper, walked beside him. They were both laughing.

"That's an odd pairing I never would have predicted," Jeff said, following her gaze to Robert and Bethany.

"It's funny, isn't it?" Tracy shook her head. Bethany couldn't be more than twenty-four, and she wore baggy clothes and dangly hoop earrings and a large bag slung over her shoulder. Her highlighted hair was piled on top of her head in a messy bun. Robert had to be at least eighty, and his button-down shirt and khaki pants were as traditional as it got. But the two of them had laughed together all throughout dinner and seemed to have struck up a friendship. "But that's what this whole evening was about. Giving people a chance to get to know one another outside of church."

Millie Ettlinger and her sister, Arielle, who was visiting from St. Louis, climbed into Millie's car in the driveway. Jeff and Tracy waved again as Millie backed into the street and drove away.

"And I'd have to say it was a success," Jeff said.

"I think it was too." Tracy watched as Bethany helped Robert into his car before walking over to hers. "It was such a fun idea, and I enjoyed getting to know so many new people."

Jeff and Tracy's house had been the third stop of a progressive dinner to welcome new attendees to Faith Church. Three groups—each a mix of new and old members—started with appetizers at Tracy's son's house then moved on to soup at Lincoln and Melody Bailey's home. They'd continued to Tracy and Jeff's for the main course. The groups started at staggered times, so Jeff and Tracy had hosted three different sets of people. Now the last group was on its way to Pastor Gary and Kathy's place, where the other two groups were waiting for them to arrive to have their dessert.

They watched as the last of their guests drove off, and then Jeff sighed. "I guess we'd better get started on that pile of dishes."

"Do we have to?" Tracy didn't even want to think about it. They must have used every dish, platter, bowl, and item of wedding china they owned tonight. She couldn't imagine how many loads they would have to put through the dishwasher. But it had been worth it.

"Unless you've hired a maid I'm not aware of, then the answer is yes," Jeff said.

Tracy sighed. "Remind me to win the lottery before our next progressive dinner. For now, we'd better get scrubbing."

She followed Jeff inside the house and filled the sink with hot, soapy water. She gently scrubbed the china pieces while Jeff put the first load of everyday dishes into the dishwasher.

"It was funny how each of the three groups had its own personality," he said as he lined up the plates in the bottom rack. "The first group was so much rowdier than the others."

"I think that was just Jana and Matt." Tracy laughed. Her sister's kids were seven and eleven. They had been cooped up inside with their new stepsiblings, Colton and Natalie, during the rainy afternoon and had way more energy than they should by Saturday evening. They had only been in the house a few minutes before Amy—their mom and Tracy's sister—sent them outside with a basketball and orders not to come inside until dinner was on the table.

"I did enjoy how they persuaded Grace to play basketball with them though." Jeff chuckled.

"That was amazing. I had no idea she could play so well," Tracy said. Grace Park was the head librarian in town, and while she was hardly shy and retiring, Tracy hadn't had a clue she could shoot a basket from anywhere on the court.

"And of course Susan and David are always great at a party."

"They are." Susan and David Willey were their daughter's in-laws. They were both outgoing and gregarious. David was always quick with a funny story, and his good-natured laugh was contagious. "Maybe that's why that group seemed so rambunctious. David did tell a lot of stories."

"That might have been it," Jeff agreed, setting several glasses in the top rack. "The second group was almost silent by contrast."

"They were not," Tracy said. "They were talking about a TV show you hadn't seen, so you tuned out."

"That's possible," Jeff admitted.

Mariella Lopez, who owned Buttermilk Bakeshop, mentioned that she had just binged the latest season, and just about everyone else in the second group, including Paula Jordan and Sara and Kevin, had as well.

"I will say the show did sound kind of interesting," Jeff said.

Tracy plunged her hands back into the warm water and started scrubbing a serving bowl. Tracy, like Jeff, hadn't seen the show, but from what she could tell, it involved a lot of period costumes and power struggles and royalty behaving badly. She'd never thought it sounded all that intriguing.

"Anyway, the third group had a completely different energy," Jeff said. He inserted a soap pod into the dishwasher, closed the door, and started the machine. Then he picked up a dish towel and took the dripping serving bowl from Tracy.

"They had lots of one-on-one conversations, like they were really getting to know one another," Tracy said. "I'm so glad Tom and Angie seemed to enjoy it."

"It was good of them to come, seeing as how they're just visiting town." Jeff set the serving bowl in the cabinet and reached for the plate Tracy had washed.

"True, but it's not like they're brand-new to the church. Tom grew up going there, and he knows pretty much everyone in town." Tom and Angie lived in Nebraska, and though they didn't make it back to Canton very often, they were hardly strangers there.

"I guess that's true." Jeff put the dry plate on the counter and reached for the next one. "All in all, it was a nice night. I have to admit, I was skeptical when you signed us up to host. I wasn't sure how it would go, but it turned out well. It was nice to see so many people."

Jeff surveyed the pile of dishes that still remained to be washed. "But before we do this again, let's please hire a maid."

Tracy laughed. "Paper plates might not have been a bad idea, in retrospect."

"Next time." Jeff grinned.

Working together, it didn't take them long to get the dishes under control. Another full dishwasher load soaked in the sink, but all the china and pots and pans had been dried and put away, and the counters were wiped down. The dining room, with its carved fireplace mantel and long table and chairs, had been restored to its normal state of welcoming elegance.

Tracy stretched her arms above her head. "Now that we've got that over with, I'm going to check out a new recipe I saw online that I want to try tomorrow."

Jeff groaned. "I can't even think about hosting another meal right now."

Tracy laughed. "Thankfully, it's just family."

Every Sunday, Tracy and Jeff hosted a family meal at their house, which had been Grandma Pearl's home until she'd passed away a couple of years ago. Amy and her new husband, Miles, and their kids often came, as did their cousin Robin and her husband, Terry, and their son, Kai. Robin's parents, Ruth and Marvin Peterson, usually made an appearance as well. Tracy and Jeff's kids, Chad and Sara, came as often as they could with their families. Plus, Tom and Angie would be there this week, and… Well, actually, now that she thought about it, it was kind of a lot of people to host. But everyone brought food, and no one felt the need to impress anyone else. It was a time to relax together and catch up.

"I'm going to read for a while," Jeff said.

"Sounds good."

Jeff walked into the first-floor guest room, which he used as an office, and Tracy went to the living room. She loved this room, with its big round turret in the corner. It felt more comfortable than most of the rest of the house, which had more formal furniture. This was the room where they came to relax and unwind, and to—

Wait. Where was her laptop? Hadn't it been in here? She frowned at the spot on the coffee table where she was pretty sure she'd left it and then looked around the rest of the room. Had she moved it? Maybe she'd left it somewhere else?

She walked through the archway into the library and checked the bookshelves and the side tables, but it wasn't there either. She searched the kitchen, then the screened porch and the pantry, though she couldn't remember using it in any of those places. Was it upstairs?

As she was about to go up the back stairs to check, Jeff walked into the kitchen, his brow furrowed. "Have you seen my laptop?"

"No. I'm looking for mine too."

"Yours is missing?" Jeff's eyes widened.

"I don't know that it's missing," she replied. "It's not where I thought I left it though."

"Mine isn't either."

"Okay, let's not panic," Tracy said, fighting the anxiety that was rising inside her. "Let's see if they're upstairs."

They both went up the back stairs and looked around—not in the office, not in Tracy's reading room, not in the guest room, not in their bedroom...

"Where are they?" Tracy was starting to get a very bad feeling. The laptops hadn't wandered off. If it was one laptop they couldn't find, that would be less concerning, but both of them were missing.

"Let's check again," Jeff said.

"They're not here," Tracy insisted.

"Let's check again, just to be sure."

Tracy stayed upstairs to search while Jeff went back to the rooms on the first floor, and then they switched. They met in the kitchen, empty-handed.

"Did someone take them tonight?" Tracy hated to even suggest it, but she couldn't think of another possibility. "They were both here before dinner, right?"

"They were," Jeff confirmed. "And they're not here now. Which means, as horrible as it is, that someone who was a guest in our home tonight must have taken them."

Tracy couldn't imagine it. Their guests were people from church. Had someone actually stolen the computers during a church event?

"What do we do?" Tracy asked.

"Let's call Ruth and Marvin," Jeff said. "They were in the last group. Maybe one of them saw the computers."

Tracy called Aunt Ruth. She and Uncle Marvin were on their way home after dessert at Pastor Gary's.

"We didn't see any laptops," Aunt Ruth said after conferring with Uncle Marvin. "Why? What happened to them?"

"That's what we're trying to figure out," Tracy said.

"How awful," Aunt Ruth said. "Keep us posted, and tell us if there's anything we can do to help, okay?"

"We will. Thanks." She hung up, and Jeff said, "Let's try Sara and Kevin. They were in the second group. Maybe they remember seeing someone move them."

Tracy called Sara, who was just getting the kids to bed. She said she hadn't seen any laptops, and seemed very concerned. "You don't think someone took them, do you?"

"I don't know," Tracy said wearily. "I hope not."

After she hung up with Sara, Jeff tried Amy, who had been in the first group. She hadn't seen the laptops—and neither had Miles or the kids.

"Let's see if we can find them with Locate," Tracy suggested.

She used the handy app to find her phone when she inevitably misplaced it, and sometimes checked it to see where Jeff's phone was so she would know if he was on his way home.

He pulled his phone from his pocket, opened the Locate app, and tapped on Devices. The laptops weren't there.

"Why aren't they showing up?" Tracy asked.

"I don't know," Jeff said. "But as much as I hate to say it, I think we need to call the police and report a theft."

"You don't think there's any chance there's another explanation?" Tracy knew she sounded desperate.

"I don't know, Tracy. I hate to think that someone from church would do this to us, but I can't think of another possibility."

Tracy nodded, though inside she fought back tears. Who could have done this to them, and why?

Chapter Two

"Dale will be on his way soon," Jeff said a few minutes later. He tucked his phone in his pocket and leaned against the counter, crossing his arms over his chest. "But it will be a little while, because he's over at the Baileys' place now."

"What happened there?" Tracy had searched the house again while Jeff was on the phone, but there was still no sign of the computers.

"They reported a theft after the last group left their place," Jeff said. "Some of Melody's jewelry has gone missing."

"Oh no." Tracy couldn't believe it. There were other victims, which meant that no amount of searching the house would unearth their laptops. Someone in one of the groups tonight had stolen from them and the Baileys. "Wait. What about Anna and Chad?" Tracy's son and daughter-in-law had hosted the appetizer course, the first stop of the evening for the groups.

"I don't know. Let's find out." Jeff dialed Chad and put the call on speaker.

"Hello?" Chad sounded distracted. Then again, he and his wife had three children under the age of five, so distracted was a permanent state of mind for Chad and Anna.

"Hi, Chad. How did everything go tonight?" Tracy could tell Jeff was trying hard to keep his voice light and upbeat.

"It went fine," Chad said. "Lots of fun. But it's the strangest thing—I'm sure I'm imagining it."

Tracy braced herself. She knew what was coming.

"Is something missing?" Jeff asked, dread in his voice.

"Anna's phone is gone. She got it a few weeks ago, and it's not here. Her ring light is gone too."

"Her what?" Jeff asked.

"That's the light she uses to brighten the room for her videos," Tracy said. Anna was a social media influencer, which Tracy hadn't realized was a job until Chad had started dating her. She made videos and wrote a blog about interior design, and she used a special round light on a collapsible stand to get the lighting right for the video and photo shoots she did.

"Exactly," Chad said. "She keeps it in her office upstairs, and no one went up there that I know of. But I guess someone must have, because it's gone."

"What about her phone? Is there any chance she misplaced it?" Tracy asked. But even as she said the words, she knew the answer. She was grasping at straws, hoping against hope that the thief hadn't touched her son's family too.

"No. It was sitting on the counter at the beginning of the night, and at the end, it was gone. I tried to use Locate to find it, but it didn't show up, which means it's been shut off. Whoever took it wanted to make sure it couldn't be tracked." Chad sighed. "It was a brand-new phone too. Hopefully our insurance will cover it, but what a pain."

"They have to turn it on at some point," Tracy said. "What good is a phone if you can't turn it on?"

"They will," Chad said. "Long enough to wipe it clean of our info so they can sell it, if they haven't already done so. Hang on. I'm going to put you on speaker so you can talk to Anna too."

"I can't figure out who would do something like this," Anna said, her voice echoing. "Everyone who came to the dinner was so nice. We had such a good time. They were people from church. How could one of them be responsible for something like this?"

"I've got bad news," Jeff said. "Your phone and ring light weren't the only things taken, I'm afraid. Our laptops are missing, and jewelry was taken from the Baileys' home."

"That's crazy. Someone used the progressive dinner as a way to clean up," Chad said.

"Was anything taken from Pastor Gary's place?" Anna asked.

"We don't know yet," Jeff said. "We should probably call them too."

"At least phones and laptops are replaceable," Anna said. "Expensive, but replaceable. I hope the jewelry that was taken wasn't too valuable or family heirlooms."

"I don't know, but I agree," Tracy said.

She knew Anna was right, that the laptop itself was replaceable, but she had some recent reporting work on the computer that she didn't want to lose. There was probably other stuff on there she needed too.

"Anyway, you should probably call the police station to report the theft," Tracy said. "Dale is at the Baileys' place now, and he's supposed to come over here after that."

"I guess that's true," Chad said. "We'll need a police report for the insurance, if nothing else."

"Hopefully they'll be able to figure out who's behind this," Jeff said. "And get our things returned."

"We'll give the station a call," Chad promised. "Let's hope they get it taken care of quickly."

"Let us know how it goes," Tracy said. "I'm so sorry this happened to you too."

As soon as they hung up, Jeff opened the Locate app on his phone again and searched for his laptop and Tracy's. Both were marked as NO LOCATION FOUND.

"They're still off," Tracy said. There was something incredibly violating about the idea that they'd invited someone into their home and the person had taken advantage of the opportunity to steal from them.

Next, Jeff dialed Pastor Gary's number and told him what had happened at the three houses. He let Pastor Gary know he was putting him on speaker, and Pastor Gary did the same so Kathy could listen.

"I'm so sorry to hear about this," Pastor Gary said. He truly did sound pained, and Tracy knew he was upset that such a thing had happened at a church event. "We haven't noticed anything missing so far at our place."

"Our phones are both accounted for, but they're so old they probably weren't worth stealing," Kathy added. "And we'd put our laptops in a drawer so they wouldn't be in the way."

"Did you check your jewelry?" Tracy asked. "Melody Bailey had some of hers taken."

"All I have that's worth anything at all is my wedding ring," Kathy said. "And it's on my finger. I'll go through the rest of my jewelry, but if any of it is missing, I won't be too sad."

"It sounds like we were lucky, but I'm so sorry to hear about what happened at the other houses," Pastor Gary said. "We'll be praying that whoever did this has a change of heart and returns your things."

"And if that doesn't happen, we'll pray that the thief is found quickly," Kathy said.

"We'll do the same," Jeff said. As he hung up, there was a knock at the door. Jeff left the room and returned with Sergeant Dale Leewright and another policeman Tracy recognized as Officer Maxwell.

"Hi, Tracy," Dale said. "I'm sorry to hear about this."

"It's a shock, that's for sure," Tracy said. "Did you hear that whoever it was hit Chad and Anna's place as well?"

"We did. We're headed there next," Officer Maxwell said.

"Can you tell us what happened?" Dale asked when they were all seated at the kitchen table. Tracy had brewed mint tea, but the officers declined.

Tracy and Jeff relayed where their computers had been before the night's festivities began and how they'd discovered them missing. They told the officers the names of the people in each of the three groups that had come through.

"Did anyone's behavior strike you as suspicious?" Dale asked.

"Now that you mention it, there was one strange moment," Jeff said. "It was while the first group was still arriving. Since everyone came in their own cars, they didn't all arrive at the same time. A few people were already here, and I went to let in some others. But as I passed the office on the way to the door, I saw Jody in there."

"Jody Bonilla?" Officer Maxwell asked, reading the name from his notes.

"That's right," Tracy said. She turned back to Jeff. "What was she doing in the office?"

"I didn't think anything of it at the time," Jeff said. "She looked around and said how beautiful the room is, and I thanked her."

"Did she touch a laptop?" Dale asked.

"Not that I saw. I went to get the door, and she left the office and wandered into the library, and pretty soon after that we all sat down to eat."

"Was that the last time you saw the laptop?" Officer Maxwell asked.

"Yes," Jeff said.

"She did excuse herself during dinner to use the bathroom, and then she was gone for kind of a long time," Tracy said. "It would have been long enough for her to go back to the office, take Jeff's laptop, and put it in her bag, which was by the front door. Also, if she'd wandered from the office to the library, as Jeff said, she would have gone through the living room, which was where my computer was. She could have grabbed it as well while she was taking her bathroom break."

"We'll speak with Jody," Dale said. "Is there anyone else who comes to mind? Or any other incident that sticks out as strange?"

"What about Caleb Presley?" Jeff asked. "I asked him what he likes to do in his spare time, and he said gaming. He's a teenage boy, so no surprise there. But then he told me he was trying to get money to build a custom computer specifically for gaming. It sounded like it would be really expensive."

"He said he was saving for one?" Tracy asked. "Or 'trying to get money' for one?"

"'Trying to get money,'" Jeff said.

"It could be just how teenagers talk," Tracy said. "But his mom did mention to me that he'd gotten in trouble at his last school."

"What kind of trouble?" Dale asked.

"I'm not sure," Tracy said. "She didn't elaborate." Caleb was fifteen, and he had attended—been dragged along to was probably more accurate—the dinner with his mother, Sharon, who had recently moved back home to Canton after her husband passed away. "We don't have any reason to believe he's involved. It's not fair to suspect him because he's an awkward kid who's into computers, wants money, and has been in trouble at school. That describes a lot of teenage boys."

"We'll be talking to everyone who attended the event tonight," Dale said. "Including Caleb. Can you think of anyone else?"

Tracy shook her head. Amy? Robert West? Uncle Marvin? Grace Park? It was so hard to imagine any of them stealing. Then again, it was hard to imagine any guest stealing from them, but clearly it had happened.

"No," Jeff said. "I'm afraid not."

"In that case, we'll head out," Dale said. "Don't worry. We'll do our best to find them. Sometimes stolen electronics end up at pawn shops or being sold online, so we'll keep an eye out. For now, we're off to Chad and Anna's."

"Thank you for coming," Tracy said. She sure hoped they would figure out who it was, and quickly. But she also hoped, with equal measure, that when they woke up in the morning they would discover that nothing was actually missing and it had all been a terrible mistake.

Chapter Three

Tracy sat in the sanctuary at church the next morning, trying to keep her mind focused on the service. Pastor Gary read Scripture, and she closed her eyes and tried to soak in the words of Psalm 91. "Whoever dwells in the shelter of the Most High will rest in the shadow of the Almighty. I will say of the Lord, 'He is my refuge and my fortress, my God, in whom I trust.'"

Tracy did trust God. She trusted that no matter what happened, He was in control. And yet, she couldn't stop thinking about the missing laptops and jewelry and phone and light. A fellow church member had walked away with thousands of dollars' worth of electronics and jewels last night.

Pastor Gary moved on to a passage from the Gospel of John, and Tracy tried to make herself focus on the words. Potted lilies in gold foil, left over from Easter, lined the chancel, brightening up the gloomy spring day. Tracy spotted Grace Park sitting a few rows back, next to Jody Bonilla, who had her sullen-faced teenage daughter on her other side. Tracy hadn't imagined it then—those two had hit it off last night. *Good for them.* But she also remembered what Jeff had said about Jody and his laptop. Could she be the one behind the thefts?

Jeannie Morrison sat with her mom, Paula, who had been in the second group last night. It was hard to imagine seventy-something

Paula in the market for electronics. Bethany Hill was there, but Tracy didn't see Millie Ettlinger or her sister Arielle. They'd both been in the third group. Millie worked part-time at Robin's antique shop and part-time at the high school.

She also didn't see Robert West or Mariella Lopez or Sharon Presley and her son Caleb. That wasn't necessarily suspicious. Tracy remembered how hard it could be to get teenagers out the door for church. *The police officers will interview everyone*, she reminded herself. She should let them do their jobs. She needed to focus on the service and trust that the truth would come to light. She would dwell in the shelter of the Most High and rest in the shadow of the Almighty.

But as hard as she tried, she couldn't stop thinking about the previous night, about what had happened when, and who could have taken the laptops.

After the service, Tracy made a beeline for Lincoln and Melody Bailey, a lovely African-American couple in their early fifties. They had been enthusiastic about being hosts of the progressive dinner, but now Tracy wondered if they regretted it. Melody gave Tracy a rueful smile as she approached.

"Hello, Tracy." Lincoln's voice was a deep baritone, and he wore a silk tie over his button-down. Lincoln most always wore suits to church, though most of the men dressed more casually.

"How are you doing?" Melody pulled Tracy into a hug, the sweet scent of her perfume enveloping them. Melody was also more formal, in a dark sheath dress, cashmere cardigan, and elegant heels.

"To be honest, I feel a bit shell-shocked," Tracy said. "It never occurred to me that something like this could happen during a church event."

"I feel the same way," Melody said. "In retrospect, I guess I should have locked up my mother's jewelry, but it honestly never occurred to me that I would have to."

"That's what was taken?" Tracy remembered Melody's mother as a deeply faithful woman with a quick wit and a hearty laugh. She'd sung in the choir at Faith Church for many years and had been a beloved member of the community.

Tracy couldn't imagine losing something so priceless. Her mom hadn't had any particularly nice pieces—she hadn't had an engagement ring, and her wedding ring was a simple gold band—but she would hate to lose them nonetheless.

"Yes. The big items were a set of diamond earrings and a ruby ring, but there were also some pearls and a few costume pieces as well," Melody said.

"I'm sorry," Tracy said.

"I just can't believe someone would do this," Melody said.

"And I can't figure out who *could* have done it, logistically," Lincoln said. "The jewelry was in our bedroom. I didn't see anyone go in there the whole night."

"Yet someone must have," Melody said. "We're going to send the police report to our insurance company. Have they had any luck with your computers or Anna's phone?"

"Not that I've heard," Tracy said. "But I'm hoping they'll dig up something soon."

When Lincoln and Melody moved to talk to Susan and David Willey, Tracy noticed that Tom and Angie were putting on their coats.

"Are you guys headed out?" she asked.

"Yes, we've got some errands to run," Angie said. She was petite, with bobbed blond hair and big blue eyes.

"Errands?" Tracy said. "Is there anything we can help you with?"

"No, not at all," Angie blurted. She was paler than usual, and exhausted, if the dark circles under her eyes were any indication. "Thank you, but no."

"Where are you going?" As she said it, Tracy flinched at how nosy it sounded.

Neither of them answered for a moment, and then Angie said, "Shopping."

"That's right. We're headed out to the shopping center outside of town," Tom said. In contrast to his wife, Tom was tall and gangly, with a mop of shaggy brown hair and big glasses.

"I love shopping, so that's what we're doing this afternoon," Angie added.

Tracy hadn't known that Angie loved shopping. But she didn't really know her cousin's wife all that well, and plenty of people enjoyed the thrill of finding a good bargain.

"Okay, well, have fun." Tracy pulled her own coat on. She could see Jeff was getting antsy, which meant it was time to get going. "You guys are coming over for family dinner tonight, right?"

"We wouldn't miss it," Angie said. "We're helping Robin make dessert later."

"Have a good afternoon." Tracy waved then said goodbye to her kids and collected Jeff.

After a lunch of broccoli cheddar soup and club sandwiches, Tracy was ready for a nap. Sadie, their goldendoodle, was already stretched out in a patch of sunlight, snoring.

"I'm going to go lie down for a bit," she said.

Jeff stared at his phone and didn't respond.

"Jeff? What is it?"

"My laptop. I checked Locate, and I got lucky. It's online right now."

"What?" Tracy peered over his shoulder. She saw an icon of a laptop surrounded by a white circle. The words *Jeff's Laptop* flashed beneath it. "It's at the shopping center," she said.

"Let's go." Jeff hopped up and grabbed his coat and keys.

Tracy followed on his heels, nap forgotten. She'd barely clicked her seat belt into place when Jeff backed out of the driveway and onto the street. Tracy held his phone. She took a screenshot, and then she kept her eyes on the app. The dot was still there, in the parking lot of the shopping center.

While Jeff drove, Tracy called Dale Leewright and told him what they'd seen.

"The shopping center out by the highway?" Dale clarified. When Tracy confirmed it, he told her he was on his way. Jeff continued to drive as quickly as he could while staying within the speed limit. It was about a ten-minute drive, but before they were halfway there, the little dot disappeared.

"It's gone," Tracy said.

"You mean it moved?" Jeff asked.

"I mean it vanished," Tracy said. "It's back to saying there's no location detected for your laptop."

"Whoever has it must have either turned it off or disabled the location services," Jeff said, stepping on the gas to make it through a yellow light. "Well, we know it was there a minute ago. Maybe the person who has it is still there."

They steered into the parking lot of the shopping center. A big grocery store anchored one corner, while a chain coffee store, several chain clothing stores, a discount store, and a hardware store filled the other half.

"The dot was in one of the rows in front of the hardware store," Tracy said. "Let's check there first."

Jeff headed toward that area of the lot and drove slowly up and down the aisles.

"What are we looking for?" she asked.

"I don't know," Jeff admitted. "Someone carrying a laptop or two?"

"That would stand out, for sure," Tracy said.

Most of the people they saw pushed shopping carts or carried shopping bags. No one appeared to be carrying laptops. Still, Jeff crept through the aisles, combing every section of the parking lot. They studied every person they saw, trying to spot any clue that might indicate who the thief was.

They were about to give up when a Canton Police Department vehicle entered the lot. Tracy called Dale again to tell him that the dot indicating the location of the laptop was gone, and where they were. Dale met them by the hardware store, and then he too drove up and down the aisles.

A few minutes later, he met them back at their car. "I don't see anything that could tell us where your stuff is. I'll walk through the lot to see if I can see any laptops through the car windows, but unless there's something in plain view, there's not a lot we can do."

"The person has probably left by now," Jeff said, disappointment in his voice.

"We'll keep searching," Dale promised. Tracy sent him the screenshot showing where the laptop had been. "And we'll get security camera footage, especially from this area of the parking lot. We may be able to see something there."

"Thank you so much for coming," Tracy said. Dale had a wife he no doubt liked spending Sundays with, and Tracy appreciated his dropping everything to come investigate the lead.

"It's no problem. I was on duty anyway," he said. "Maxwell and I were talking to some dinner attendees when I got your call."

"Have you learned anything?" Jeff asked.

"I couldn't tell you even if I had," Dale said. "But the truth is, no. So far we've only spoken to your aunt and uncle, and they didn't seem to have any information."

"Yeah, I don't think Aunt Ruth is really the laptop-thief type," Tracy said.

"This was a good lead. With any luck, the security footage will give us a new direction to explore," Dale said.

It wasn't until they were back in the car and driving home that Tracy dared to voice the fear that rattled around in her mind.

"You didn't see Tom and Angie's car in the lot, did you?" she asked. They'd driven Tom's black SUV from Lincoln. Tracy had seen it parked behind Robin's shop a few days before.

"No," Jeff said. "Why?"

Tracy realized he hadn't been with her when she'd spoken to them after church. "They said they were going to the shopping center straight from church."

Jeff kept his hands on the wheel, focused on the road ahead. "I didn't see any cars with a Nebraska license plate in the lot."

"I didn't either," Tracy said.

"Maybe they finished up their shopping quickly and left," Jeff said.

"Yeah, you're probably right," Tracy said.

But something didn't sit well with her. How would they have finished their shopping already, especially if Angie enjoyed it as much as she claimed? Jeff and Tracy hadn't been home from church for very long. And Angie had been a bit cagey when Tracy asked about her afternoon plans. Perhaps it was simply that she was tired.

"You don't think there's any way they had anything to do with this, do you?" Jeff asked.

"No," Tracy said immediately. Tom was family.

Still, it was odd that they'd said they were coming to the same place where the laptop had come online briefly and that their car wasn't there when they'd said it would be. But surely there was a good reason for that. She would ask her cousin about it when he came over for dinner. There had to be a good explanation.

Chapter Four

Tracy's phone rang while she chopped vegetables to go with a pot roast. She had been unsettled all afternoon, and it felt strange not to have her laptop on hand. More than once she'd had a thought and wanted to research something and then remembered her computer was gone and had to use her phone instead. She hadn't realized how much she'd come to rely on it.

She set down the knife, wiped her hands on a dish towel, and picked up the phone, hoping it was Dale Leewright calling. But the screen read JEANNIE MORRISON.

"Hi, Jeannie," Tracy said. "How is everything?"

"It's all right," Jeannie said. "The kids are with their dad for spring break, so it's too quiet around here, but other than that, things are good. Mom said she had a good time at the progressive dinner, though we were both sorry to hear about the items that went missing. The police were here to ask her about it this afternoon. I hope they're recovered soon."

"Thank you," Tracy said. "Me too."

"The thing is, after the police left, Mom went to make a call on her cell phone, but she couldn't find it," Jeannie said.

"Oh dear." Had the thief taken Paula's phone too?

"Mom is convinced someone stole the phone, but I don't want to jump to any conclusions, so I'm calling around to the places from last night and asking if anyone has seen it. You're the last host I've called, so if you don't have it, I think the next thing I need to do is call the people who were at the dinner to ask if they saw her use it or if they might have picked it up by accident."

"We don't have it," Tracy said. "I honestly don't remember seeing your mother with a cell phone at all."

"She doesn't use it very much," Jeannie said. "She usually keeps it in her bag, and to be honest, half the time she lets it run out of battery. Which appears to be the case at the moment, because it's not showing up on Locate."

"If someone took it, they could have turned it off," Tracy suggested.

"Yes, I suppose that's possible," Jeannie said. "It's a few years old, so I'm not sure how long it holds a charge, but in any case, we don't have it, and we can't see where it is."

"Was it in her bag last night?" Tracy asked.

"She said she took it out at your place to take a picture of the wallpaper in the library. She wants to get similar paper for her room."

"I can help her with that." Though Tracy and Jeff had updated a lot of the decor since they'd inherited the house from Grandma Pearl, they hadn't touched the floral-patterned paper Grandma had hung when she'd moved into the house. Now it was so old-fashioned it was back in style.

"And she says she put it in her bag by the front door after that, but it wasn't there this afternoon."

Tracy couldn't imagine not using her phone for most of a day and night. If it went missing, she'd know right away. Then again, Paula's generation wasn't used to them—or dependent on them—in the same way her daughter's generation was.

"I haven't seen it, but I'll tell Jeff, and we'll definitely keep an eye out for it," Tracy said. "I'm pretty sure it's not here though. We scoured the place looking for the missing laptops."

"Thank you." Jeannie sighed. "If it doesn't turn up soon, I guess I'll call the police and report it missing as well."

"I'll pray that you find it," Tracy said. "Please let me know if you do."

"Of course. Have a good night, Tracy."

Tracy couldn't believe there had been another theft last night—and from one of the guests, which was a first. What else was taken? Would they discover that others besides the hosts and Paula were missing their belongings?

She tried to keep her mind on positive thoughts, and to further that effort, she listened to some worship music while she cooked. By the time Jana and Matt came running in with Colton and Natalie, while Amy and Miles trailed behind them at a more sedate pace, Tracy was in better spirits. She smiled when she saw Miles touch Amy's back gently as they walked into the room together.

A moment later, Robin and Terry arrived with Kai, and then Sara and Kevin showed up with Aiden and Zoe, and soon the whole house was full of noisy chaos, exactly the way Tracy liked it. Anna and Chad came in with their three kids—Corbin, Emerson, and baby Elizabeth—and Tom and Angie came with Aunt Ruth and Uncle Marvin. They all gathered at the table, Jeff said grace, and everyone dug into heaping servings of pot roast, rolls, scalloped potatoes, and green beans with bacon. The conversation naturally shifted toward the thefts.

"How much do you think those items would be worth, if someone tried to sell them?" Aunt Ruth asked as she speared a green bean with her fork.

"I have no idea," Tracy said. "Obviously enough to make it worth the risk to someone."

"You said some laptops went missing, right? Maybe someone wanted an extra screen for gaming," Kai said. "A lot of people use two monitors. I'd love a second one, but Mom won't let me have one."

"I'm so mean," Robin said, shaking her head. "I won't let my teenager have two computers so he can play video games all day."

"I only need a second monitor, not a second computer," Kai protested, scooping up his last bite of potatoes.

"The answer is no," Robin said. "Now, why don't you take your cousins outside?"

Kai pushed back his chair, and the other kids—except for Elizabeth, of course—followed suit. He helped the youngest ones carry their plates to the kitchen before herding them all outside.

Tracy glanced around the table. Most everyone was finished, though Angie had hardly touched her food. She'd eaten part of a dinner roll, but as far as Tracy could tell, she'd done little more than pick at the rest of her food.

"Someone planning to sell the laptops seems the most likely scenario to me," Tom said. "There's always a market for used electronics, and it would be an easy way to make some quick cash."

"That sounds right," Miles said, "but there are lots of other ways someone might be able to use a laptop, especially if it isn't password protected."

"Mine isn't," Tracy confessed.

"It's not?" Sara said. "Why in the world wouldn't you put a password on it, Mom?"

"Mom, you should have a password," Chad scolded. "It's important."

"It never occurred to me someone might steal it," Tracy said in her defense.

"Once a thief gets into your computer, they have access to your passwords, financial information, emails, shopping habits, home security system—and that's off the top of my head," Kevin said. "It's startling when you think about how much information we put on our devices these days."

Tracy realized he was right. She did her banking on her laptop, paid her credit card bills, and logged into all kinds of websites. The thief could easily find all of that. Her browser even stored the passwords to those websites so she didn't have to remember them. If she ever got her computer back, she'd add a password to her lock screen.

"It's probably a good idea to monitor your bank accounts and credit cards for the next few days," Kevin said. He worked at a bank, so he knew what he was talking about. "The same thing is true for your phone," he added to Anna. "I imagine you have apps for your bank and credit card on your phone?"

"Yes." Anna ate with one hand and held six-month-old Elizabeth in her lap with the other. "But my phone has facial recognition as a security protection, so hopefully whoever has it won't be able to get into it."

Tracy had seen the feature on newer phones. The user simply held the phone in front of their face to unlock it. If the phone didn't recognize them, it wouldn't unlock.

"Let's hope so," Chad said. "Though based on the research I did today, there are ways to get around that and get into the phone if the thief is tech savvy."

"Which would rule out most of the people who participated in the progressive dinner," Aunt Ruth said.

"Most of them," Tracy agreed. "But not all of them."

"There's Caleb," Kevin said. "Sharon's son. He was in the second group with us."

"He's the best bet for tech savvy," Jeff agreed. "We thought of him as a potential suspect, but aside from his comfort with technology, we don't have any reason to distrust him."

"He didn't say much to anyone all night," Sara said. "Until we started talking about a TV show he likes."

"There also wasn't anyone else his age around," Tracy pointed out. "It couldn't have been fun to be the lone teenager surrounded by a bunch of adults."

"He probably didn't have a lot to say to us old people," Sara said with a laugh.

Tracy laughed along with her. Sara was in her late twenties. Still, that was a big difference from fifteen.

"Fair enough," Kevin agreed.

"Sharon was in my class in high school," Robin said. "She was really nice. She loved reading, and it was obvious that English was her favorite subject. She always had a book in her hand."

"Sounds like someone else I know." Jeff nudged Tracy with a grin.

"True," Robin said. "But she was really quiet too, like Caleb."

"Anyone else?" Tracy asked.

"What about Arielle?" Amy suggested. "Millie's sister."

Tracy remembered Arielle as quiet and shy. She was younger than Millie, probably in her mid to late twenties, with long brown hair and glasses.

"Did she do anything suspicious?" Jeff asked.

"No," Amy said. "Not that I saw. She simply seemed reluctant to tell us anything about herself. Melody asked her about what she does for work and for fun, and she didn't really have an answer to either. But that's not exactly suspicious, I guess."

"She came off as kind of shy to me," Anna said kindly.

"From what Millie told me, Arielle's visit wasn't planned," Robin said. Tracy was glad Robin was speaking up, as she knew Millie the best of all of them. "Millie had signed up for the dinner, and when Arielle called and said she was coming home for a visit, Millie signed her up to come along. So I think it's fair to say she was more or less roped into it, kind of like Caleb was. And if she's shy, meeting that many people all at once might have been overwhelming for her."

"Did anyone learn anything about her?" Chad asked.

"I heard her say she was visiting from St. Louis," Sara said. "But that's about it."

"Well, she wasn't particularly talkative, but that doesn't make her guilty," Tracy said. "We're trying to come up with people who actually behaved suspiciously."

"There's Jody Bonilla," Jeff said. He explained to the group how he'd found her in the office.

"She did the same thing at my house," Anna said. "I walked into the kitchen and found her looking at my phone."

"What?" Amy sucked in a breath. "You mean she picked it up and was looking at it?"

"No, she didn't pick it up. It was on the table, and she was bent over, looking at it. She must have waked it up, though, because she saw the wallpaper picture of the kids and commented on how cute they are. She recognized that it was a newer model and said how jealous she was. I thought it was strange at the time. I mean, who touches someone else's phone?"

"And there was the fact that she went to the bathroom and took a long time," Jeff said.

"She did that here too?" Chad asked. "It was the same story at our place. She excused herself from the table to use the bathroom, and then was gone for a long time."

"Long enough to swipe a phone and a ring light or a couple of laptops," Amy said.

"Don't forget the jewelry," Tracy said.

"My light folds up really small," Anna said. "I bought it because it was convenient and portable. I never imagined how that would make it easier to steal."

"Maybe she had some health issue," Uncle Marvin said.

"Maybe," Robin said, her tone skeptical. "Does anyone know anything about her?"

"I think she said she moved home after a divorce," Anna said. "She has a teenage daughter and works at the hospital as a nurse, if I remember correctly."

"Okay," Aunt Ruth said. "Well, she's on the list. Who else?"

Tracy glanced over at Tom. He and Angie had been quiet during the whole discussion. She couldn't really think he had done it. But she couldn't deny the blip on Locate while he and Angie were supposed to be at the shopping center. And since they had mentioned Jody disappearing into the bathroom, Tracy suddenly recalled that Angie had also made two trips to the bathroom in the time she'd been at their house.

"Have you noticed that all of the people on the list are new to town?" Terry said. "That's not very welcoming or hospitable of us."

"I guess you're right," Robin answered.

"That's because none of the people we know would do this to us," Aunt Ruth said. "None of our friends would steal from their neighbors like this."

"Perhaps it truly was one of the new members," Terry continued. "I don't know. I wanted to point it out because of what Jesus said about welcoming the stranger and all that."

Tracy felt chastened, and she could see that Amy did too. It was unfair to assume that only the new people could have been behind the thefts. But at the same time, Aunt Ruth was right. It was hard to see how someone they knew could have done such a thing.

"What about Bethany Hill?" Anna suggested. "When she was at our place, she kept disappearing."

"She did, didn't she?" Uncle Marvin agreed.

"She's not new," Aunt Ruth added.

"Now that you mention it, it happened here too," Jeff said. "While everyone was chatting before we sat down to eat, she stepped out of the room with her phone. It happened again when Tracy and I were gathering everyone's plates after the meal."

The observations jogged Tracy's memory. "I thought something was going on with her private life, and I didn't want to intrude. Now that you mention it, I didn't see where she went either time."

"She could have scoped things out the first time then gone back and taken the things the second time," Jeff murmured, as if he didn't want to say it.

Tracy wanted to argue that it was impossible. She worked with Bethany at the newspaper. She was a nice kid, a few years out of college, very bright and eager and a hard worker. She couldn't be behind the thefts. But then Tracy recognized that she was falling into the trap that Terry had mentioned.

"And she had that huge bag," Aunt Ruth continued. "What does anybody do with a bag that size?"

"Oversize bags are very in, Aunt Ruth," Sara said.

"Well, you could fit a whole person inside hers." Aunt Ruth sniffed.

Miles laughed. "I'm pretty sure there weren't any people missing after the event."

"My point is that she could easily have snuck a laptop or two in there, never mind Anna's light and some jewelry."

Tracy realized she was right. It didn't mean Bethany had anything to do with it, but technically she could have. She had means and opportunity.

The conversation remained on the topic of the thefts for a few more minutes, but no new suspects or theories came up.

When the room grew quiet, Tracy said, "Who's ready for dessert?"

Jeff and Tom hopped up to clear away the dinner plates, but when Tom reached forward to grab Robin's plate, she stopped him.

"Hang on." Robin bit her lip, studying his wrist. An awkward pause stretched, and Tracy tried to figure out what had caught her attention. "Can I see your watch?"

"Sure." Tom set the plates on the table and unhooked the silver links of his watch from around his wrist. He handed it over for her examination.

Seeing it, Tracy was filled with nostalgia. It had originally been Grandpa Howard's watch, and when he died, it had passed to her father. Dad had worn that watch every day while Tracy was growing up, and the sight of it made her miss him all over again. But she smiled at Tom. She missed Dad, but seeing his watch made her feel close to him again. It was an antique Rolex, and she was under the impression that it was valuable. Since Dad hadn't had any sons, he'd willed the watch to his nephew.

"Tom, what happened to the watch?" Robin asked.

Tom's brow furrowed. "What do you mean?"

Robin rubbed her finger over the glass face. Then she flipped the watch over and examined the back. "This isn't Uncle Noah's watch."

Tom narrowed his eyes. "What are you talking about? It's the same watch I got after the funeral."

"No." Robin shook her head. "I'm afraid it's not. It's not a real Rolex."

"What are you saying?" Tom asked.

"I'm sorry, but it's not. This lens over the date is supposed to be convex on a Rolex. It's called a Cyclops lens, and it magnifies the date portion of the watch face. But this one is flat. And given its age, the face should be acrylic, but this one is glass."

"Wait. You can tell the watch is fake because it has a nicer face?" Amy asked.

Robin nodded. "I got to know a dealer who was really into watches a few years back, and he taught me a lot about Rolexes. The original watch was from the 1950s, right?"

"I think so," Amy said.

"That sounds right," Tracy said.

"They used acrylic up until the seventies," Robin said. "Since this watch has a glass face, we know it was made after that. Plus, the serial number here?" She pointed to something Tracy couldn't see from across the table, but Tom leaned over to peer at it. "On a Rolex, that number would be deeply engraved into the metal, but you can see this is merely etched on with acid." She flipped it back over. "You can also tell because the movement of the hands is jerky. It should be perfectly smooth."

"So you're saying the watch is a fake?" Tom repeated.

"I'm afraid so," Robin said. "I'm sure you inherited the real one, but it must have been switched at some point. I can't say when, because I'm not sure I would have noticed a fake before the last couple of years, but I can tell you for sure this watch isn't a real Rolex."

"How is that possible?" Tom asked, his face stricken.

"And what happened to Dad's Rolex?" Aunt Ruth chimed in.

"I don't know," Robin said, shaking her head. "But I can tell you that this isn't it."

Chapter Five

When Tracy got to work Monday morning, she tried to make herself focus. Each week, she wrote a column for the *Lewis County Times* in which she explored a forgotten piece of local history. Last week she'd started working on a piece about the history of Tully, a town north of Canton that was destroyed when the Mississippi overran its banks in 1851.

Tracy opened her folder of notes and tried to write, but all she could think about was the missing items. Though she knew it was futile, she opened the Locate app on her phone and checked whether her laptop came up on the list of devices. NO LOCATION FOUND.

She turned back to the computer the paper had loaned her, but instead of researching her article, she opened a new search window and typed in *Pawn Shops Canton MO*. She knew there was one on the outskirts of Canton and several more in Quincy. Her current search revealed their addresses, and she jotted them down in a notebook. Dale had suggested that the laptops might end up at a pawn shop or for sale online. She supposed an auction site was the most likely place to sell electronics online. It wouldn't hurt to take a quick peek.

She opened another tab and pulled up a popular auction site. She typed the model of her laptop in the search bar. Dozens of computers identical to hers appeared for sale. Some listings showed photos of the laptops with the original packaging, and others depicted what were clearly used machines that were posed on beds or desks in peoples' homes. But the laptops all seemed the same. How was she supposed to know which one was hers—if any of them were? Her computer didn't have any distinguishing characteristics that she could think of. She hadn't added any decals or stickers or marked it in any way.

She twisted to face Jake, who wrote about sports at the desk next to hers. She'd learned over the years that if she needed help with a website or technology of some kind, asking someone born at least a decade after her was often the easiest solution. He was currently bobbing his head to whatever music played in his earbuds.

"Jake."

He pushed the button on his earbud to pause the music. "What's up?"

"Do you know how to figure out where someone is selling an item from?"

"Sure. Click on it."

She clicked on the picture of the first listing, and he pointed at the top of the screen, where it gave a location.

"San Bernadino, California," Tracy said. "Okay. What if I want to see laptops that are being sold from Missouri?" She had no idea how far the thief could have gotten, but she had to start somewhere.

"Easy enough. Scroll down." He got up and came over to her desk. He tapped a section on the page that had buttons for different filters and directed her to one labeled ITEM LOCATION. From there, a window popped up that allowed her to choose the state or to show listings within a certain radius of a particular zip code. She chose to search for listings within fifty miles of Canton, and three results came up.

"When you click on them, you can check out the different seller profiles," Jake said. "That might tell you more about them."

Tracy thanked him, and Jake went back to his own work as Tracy clicked on the first listing.

Someone with the screen name ZappoD in Quincy, Illinois, was selling a laptop advertised as new, though the photos showed scuffs and marks on the keys. DellaBarone1 was selling a used laptop from Edina, Missouri, and the photo showed the computer on a floral bedspread. A third laptop was for sale in Nauvoo, Illinois, from a CatQueen336.

Were any of them hers? She clicked on the seller who appeared to be a cat lover to see if they were trying to unload anything else—another laptop, perhaps, or a new phone and ring light. But the lone items they had for sale were the laptop, a glittery case for a newer model smartphone, and tickets to a pop concert that summer. DellaBarone1 had nothing but the laptop for sale, and ZappoD appeared to sell laptops of every model, but no phones or anything else.

She didn't think she could rule any of them out, but she also couldn't tell if any of them belonged to her.

"Hi, Tracy." Bethany Hill stood over her with a large to-go cup in her hand.

"Hey, Bethany."

"I wanted to say thanks again for Saturday night. It was a lot of fun."

"I'm so glad you were able to come," Tracy said. "It was a fun night, wasn't it?"

"Hey, were you guys hanging out without me?" Jake took out his earbuds and sent them a goofy grin.

"We sure were." Bethany laughed. "It was the best party in town."

"And I wasn't on the list?"

Tracy couldn't be sure, but the way Jake gazed at Bethany made her suspect that he might have a bit of a crush. Now that she thought about it, he had been wearing fewer old T-shirts and more polos and button-downs recently. He'd even cut his hair a few weeks ago. She tried to hide her own grin.

"You're welcome any time," Bethany said. "It was a church event. You can come on over to church."

"That's not really my thing." Jake popped his earbuds back into his ears, but Tracy noticed he didn't stop watching Bethany from the corner of his eye.

"Anyway," Bethany said to Tracy, "I heard about the stuff that was stolen. I'm so sorry. The police talked to me yesterday, and I told them everything I know. I keep racking my brain, thinking I must have seen something, or someone acting suspicious, but I can't think of anything."

Tracy considered her. She sounded genuine. But Tracy couldn't ignore what had come up at dinner the previous night, how Bethany had stepped away from the group at each of the houses, and about the size of her bag.

"Did you see the laptops at our house?" Tracy felt strange sitting while Bethany stood over her, so she grabbed the rolling chair from the empty desk next to hers for Bethany to sit in.

Bethany lowered herself into it and shook her head. "I don't think so. If I did, it didn't register, you know?"

"What about Anna's phone? Did you see that?" Tracy decided not to mention Paula's phone. She didn't think many people had heard about that theft yet, so if Bethany revealed that she knew about it, she would be tipping her hand.

"Again, if I did, I didn't register it," she said. "And I definitely didn't see Melody's jewelry. That's so strange to me. Who would go into her room and go through her jewelry box and take her personal things? I mean, a phone is one thing, but her mother's ring is something else entirely."

Tracy thought about that. On one hand, there wasn't really any difference between stealing a phone and stealing jewelry. Both items were valuable, and both actions were violations of someone's trust. But she could also see what Bethany meant. Phones and laptops were ubiquitous and were merely tools, whereas family heirlooms were more personal and held more sentimental value.

"Did you see anyone acting strangely?" Tracy asked.

"I mean, I don't know everyone in the group super well, but I was mostly surprised at how good we all got along. I was worried at first, because I really didn't know anyone in my group. But everyone was so great. I found out Angie is an ER doc, which is amazing. I could never do that. Millie was so funny with her stories about the kids at school. And did you know Robert West ran the ferry back and forth across the Mississippi for decades?"

"I noticed you and Robert hit it off," Tracy said.

"He's so cool. He reminds me of my grandpa, who died a few years ago."

"Then I'm even happier that you and Robert connected."

"Anyway, it was more fun than I thought it would be." The smile fell from Bethany's face. "I can't imagine anyone in our group taking your stuff."

"I can't either." Tracy sighed. "The thing is, I can't imagine anyone in any group being behind it, but someone must have been."

"Let me know if there's any way I can help," Bethany said. "I sure hope they find your things."

"Thank you, Bethany. I appreciate it." Tracy hated to ruin what was such a friendly chat, but she knew she couldn't miss the opportunity to see what Bethany had to say about her disappearances from the group during the meal. "By the way, was everything okay on Saturday?"

"What do you mean?" Bethany crossed her legs and pulled on the hem of her sweater. Tracy couldn't tell if she was fidgeting or trying to get comfortable.

"You seemed a bit distracted," Tracy said. "And I noticed you left the room a few times with your phone."

Did Tracy imagine it, or did Bethany hesitate a moment too long before she said, "I was hoping no one would notice, and I'm sorry if I was rude."

"I'm not concerned with that. I just want to make sure everything is okay." It was mostly true.

"Yeah, it's just this thing with my roommate." Bethany grimaced. "She told me Saturday she's moving out next weekend. Now I have to find another roommate—before next month's rent is due. And she still owes me rent from this month, so I was kind of freaking out. We were in the middle of a texting argument, and I left the room a few times to respond to messages from her."

The explanation sounded plausible enough. Was it true though? And if it was, that meant Bethany was worried about money, which gave her even more motive to have taken the valuable items.

"I'm sorry to hear that," Tracy said. "Did you get it figured out?"

"Not really," Bethany said. "She's still refusing to pay what she owes me, so it is what it is. I'm trying to trust God. I know He'll work it out for good, as He always does."

"You can say that again," Tracy said. "I'm trying to do the same about the stolen items."

"Well, I should get to work. Those classifieds won't proof themselves." Bethany pushed herself up. "But I wanted to say thanks, and again, I'm sorry if I was rude."

"You have nothing to apologize for, but thank you, Bethany. I appreciate it."

Both Tracy and Jake watched as Bethany returned the chair to the empty desk and walked to her desk at the front of the big open newsroom. She'd had the opportunity, and she had a motive—she was in financial trouble. She also had the means—a giant bag. But would she be talking about trusting God's plan if she was a thief? Tracy smiled at Jake, and he quickly turned back to his computer screen.

Tracy resumed work on her column. She got a few paragraphs written, but after her conversation with Bethany, she was having an even harder time focusing.

"Tracy?" Eric Watson, the paper's editor-in-chief, stood behind her. She turned to face him. He wore a slim blue suit, and his brown hair had grown out a bit longer than usual. She hadn't heard him leave his office.

"Hi, Eric. What can I do for you?"

"Can you get a story about the budget dispute over at the Canton sanitation department ready for this week's paper?"

"Sure." Very few things sounded drier than a story about the finances of garbage collection, but if Eric wanted a story about it, she would get him one. "Is there anyone in particular you want me to talk to?"

"Joe Rivers is the head of the department. Get a statement from him and from someone on the city council," Eric said. "We could use about fifteen hundred words."

"Will do."

Tracy shrugged into her light coat and grabbed her notebook and her purse. She'd better get cracking if the story was going to be ready for this week's edition. She walked out into the bright spring sunshine. The dogwoods along the street were in full bloom, the pink blossoms gorgeous against the deep blue sky. Daffodils and tulips brightened the beds at the bases of the trees, and the air was crisp, but it carried a hint of warmer days ahead. After a long, cold Midwestern winter, spring had arrived.

Tracy walked toward Lincoln Bailey's office. He was on the city council, and she could start by talking to him. Lincoln's office was above Pop Rocks Vintage, a cute boutique that was always full of retro finds. She climbed the carpeted interior stairs to the second floor, walking past black-and-white photos of Canton from different moments in history.

When she stepped into the office, she found Lincoln's administrative assistant, Marie, behind the receptionist's desk.

"Hi, Tracy," Marie said, smiling. "How are you?"

"I'm all right." Tracy held up her notebook. "I'm working on a piece about the sanitation department. I was hoping I could get a quote from Lincoln."

"I'm sure he'd love nothing more than to talk about garbage with you." Marie laughed. "I'll see if he's free." She pushed herself up, crossed the room, and knocked lightly on Lincoln's door. When she heard a faint "Yes?" she opened the door and went inside.

Tracy eyed the chairs in the waiting area, hoping she wouldn't be there long.

A moment later, Marie came back out and gestured to Tracy. "He's available."

"Thank you." Tracy stepped inside the light-filled office. Lincoln's college and law school diplomas hung on the wall, along with more vintage photos of Canton. Lincoln was seated behind his large desk, and he stood as she walked inside.

"Hi, Tracy. Marie tells me you're here to talk garbage." He gestured for her to sit.

"I'm working on a story about the budget cuts at the sanitation department," Tracy said, taking the chair across the desk from him. "I was hoping you could give me a quote."

"Sure. 'The city council is working hard to resolve this matter in a manner that is beneficial to all parties.'"

She jotted it down. "Very diplomatic."

"Was Joe Rivers as diplomatic?" he asked, a wry smile on his face.

"I haven't spoken to him yet," Tracy said. "I guess you'll have to read Wednesday's paper to find out."

"I guess I will." Lincoln leaned forward. "Now, if we're done discussing garbage, can you tell me if you've heard any news about Saturday night's thefts?"

"I haven't," Tracy said. "I know the police are investigating it and talking to everyone who attended the dinner, but I haven't heard any updates."

"We haven't either," Lincoln said. "And we've been going over it again and again, trying to figure out who could have gone upstairs without us noticing."

"Did you come up with anyone?" Tracy asked.

"The one person we could remember disappearing for any amount of time was Jody," Lincoln said. "She excused herself to go to the bathroom right as that group was sitting down, and she was gone for a while."

"That's odd," Tracy said. "She did the same thing at our place." *Another strike against Jody.*

"Well, that might mean something, or it might not." Lincoln shrugged. "We've also been trying to dig up pictures of the missing jewelry, like the police suggested. We found this photo of Melody's mother wearing the ruby ring." He pulled out his phone, tapped the screen a few times, then handed it to her.

The photo depicted a beautiful bronze-skinned woman wearing a purple dress and matching church hat decorated with flowers and tulle. She held a plate of cake in the church's fellowship hall, and her head was thrown back in laughter. On her right hand, she wore an ornate gold ring with a teardrop-shaped ruby surrounded by small diamonds.

"This was taken at Melody's parents' when they celebrated their fiftieth wedding anniversary. Her husband gave her the ring on their twenty-fifth anniversary."

"It's beautiful," Tracy said. "And obviously irreplaceable for its sentimental value. I sure hope you get it back."

"Me too." Lincoln cocked his head. "Are you working with the police on this one?"

Tracy laughed. "You mean, am I trying to solve it myself?"

"Feel free to interpret that question however you like."

"Once again, very diplomatic."

Lincoln merely smiled.

"So far, I've checked into what the thief might have done with the stolen goods," Tracy said. "I'm leaving it to the police to interview the potential suspects." But even as she said it, she knew it wasn't technically true. Wasn't that what she'd been doing when she spoke to Bethany earlier?

"Well, thanks for your help," she said, pushing herself to her feet.

"Anytime," Lincoln said. "And you'll let me know if you discover anything, won't you?"

Tracy grinned. "Will do."

As she left his office, she only hoped she had something to report to Lincoln—and soon.

Chapter Six

Tracy said goodbye to Marie, went downstairs, and started to walk back toward the newspaper office to get her car. She'd have to drive to the sanitation department office. But as she passed Robin's antique shop, Pearls of Wisdom, Robin came running out, calling her name.

Tracy smiled at her cousin. Her long dark hair was scooped up into a ponytail, and she wore her favorite aqua sweater. "What's up? Or are you just really that excited to see me?"

"Tom and I were talking about you, and here you are."

"Tom is here?"

"He's inside." Robin gestured for her to come into the shop. "We have a question for you."

Tracy followed Robin through the door and into the antique shop, which was filled with an ever-changing collection of finds. Today at the front of the store was a set of low-slung armchairs covered in deep blue linen-like fabric set around a cherrywood coffee table with scrolled legs. A teapot and matching cups painted with pink flowers sat on the coffee table, which was also staged with several leather-bound books.

"This is nice." Tracy touched one of the chairs. All the display needed was a cozy fireplace.

"Careful. That chair is worth more than some small cars."

"What?" Tracy yanked her hand away. She eyed the chair, noting its simple curved back and plain wooden legs. "What is it doing here?"

"I'm hoping to sell it." Robin laughed. "This is a store, you'll remember."

"I didn't think people around here spent that much on furniture."

"Some of them do." Robin shrugged. "Anyway, come on. Tom is over here. Any news on the laptops?"

"I'm afraid not," Tracy said.

When they reached the counter, Tracy waved to Millie Ettlinger, who smiled and waved back. At the rear of the store, they found Tom hunched over the fake Rolex, which was sitting on a glass case of watches and jewelry.

"I asked Tom to bring the watch in so I could examine it with my loupe," Robin said, holding up a cylindrical-shaped magnifying glass. "I was trying to see if there were any identifying marks or another way to determine where this came from, but I haven't had any luck with that, sadly."

"We want to figure out when the watch was switched out, and so we thought we might try to see if there was any way to establish that the watch was an original Rolex when Grandpa got it," Tom said. "So there are no questions about that."

"Authentic Rolexes come with papers," Robin explained. "And since the papers are not with the watch, we figured that if they exist, there's only one place they could be." She raised her eyebrows at Tracy.

Tracy laughed. "I understand. You're welcome to swing by our house anytime and poke around in the attic." The attic of Grandma

Pearl's house—now Tracy and Jeff's house—was stuffed full of family treasures and long-forgotten items. The family was making headway cleaning it out and organizing it, but it was an ongoing project. "Text me and Jeff when you're coming so you don't give one of us a heart attack if we hear someone walking around upstairs. You have your key, right?"

"I do." Robin nodded. "Thanks, Tracy."

"Of course. I hope you find what you're looking for."

Tracy threaded her way through the store to the front and stepped back out into the spring sunshine. Her stomach growled, and she realized it was lunchtime.

She ducked into Café Chew, a great little sandwich shop, bought a turkey and cheese on rye, and then sat on a bench under an oak tree to eat it. While she ate, she scrolled through emails on her phone. She'd received a few suggestions for her column and a couple of comments from Annette on a story she'd submitted on Friday. Nothing that couldn't wait.

Tracy finished her sandwich, tossed the wrapper in the garbage can on the corner, and made her way to the parking lot behind the newspaper to get her car. She drove through the small town, past the cheery storefronts and historic homes. It didn't take long before she was out of the historic district and driving toward the highway.

The sanitation department was in a low cinder-block building surrounded by a wide parking lot. Several garbage trucks were in the lot. Tracy walked inside and conducted a quick interview with the department head, Joe Rivers, who told her about what the budget dispute meant for the residents of Canton. A few minutes later, she walked out, satisfied she had enough to write her story.

Sitting in her car, though, she hesitated. She should go back to the office and get the article written so Annette could edit it. But the pawn shop in Canton was one short block away. She decided to make a stop there first, so she drove around the strip mall on the next block until she found the place tucked into a rear corner. Tracy parked in front and walked in uncertainly.

Inside, the walls were lined with shelves displaying televisions, computers, and other electronics. Golf clubs leaned against one wall, and another section featured bikes and lawn mowers. A glass case held an impressive collection of gold chains, wedding bands, and diamond earrings. Tracy stopped and leaned over the case, wondering if she might spot Melody's earrings. She scanned the few sets on display, but she had no idea how to identify Melody's. She examined the collection of rings, and none of them resembled the ruby ring in the picture Lincoln had shown her.

"Hello." A man with a full brown beard and a sleeve of tattoos greeted her with a warm smile. He stood behind a plexiglass counter that exhibited silver lighters and pocketknives. "How can I help you?"

"I'm searching for a few things," she said. "A couple of laptops, a phone, a ring light, and some jewelry."

"Are you interested in buying these items?" he asked.

"No," Tracy said. "They've gone missing, and we thought there was a chance they might wind up at a pawn shop."

"I see." He offered his hand. "I'm Mitch."

She shook it. "Tracy."

"A lot of people think pawn shops are where thieves unload stolen goods, but the truth is that we work really hard to make sure everything in our shop is legit."

"What do you mean?"

"Basically, I make loans. If someone needs quick cash—say, a hundred dollars to make rent this month—they bring in something they own, and I tell them how much I can loan them for it. If they come back within the month and pay off the loan with interest, the item is theirs again. If they come back but don't have all the cash, I can extend the loan. If they don't come back at all, I keep the item and sell it. As you can see, we have a lot of fine merchandise. Everything out here is for sale." He gestured toward the wall of computers, DVD players, video game consoles, and televisions. "The electronics are over there." The fluorescent lights overhead popped and hummed.

"So these are all items that someone gave you in exchange for a loan and didn't come back for?" Tracy clarified.

"Or things people have sold to us outright. Sometimes people prefer to do that. The stuff we're waiting for owners to collect is in another room." Mitch jerked a thumb over his shoulder to a door marked EMPLOYEES ONLY.

Tracy felt a wave of sadness over once-treasured items that had to be given up in exchange for quick cash. She knew how desperate she would have to be to part with her wedding ring. She would sell pretty much everything else first. And nothing would stop her from coming back to reclaim it. What had happened to stop the owners from returning for their property? She was surrounded by evidence of people in seemingly hopeless situations. Tracy said a quick prayer for them, wherever they were, that they would know God's love and comfort.

"If I buy an item—say a laptop—and it turns out to be stolen, I'm out of luck if the police show up," Mitch continued. "If they can prove it was stolen, they take it and return it to the original owner. I lose my money and the laptop. I can also be charged with receiving stolen merchandise. I don't like it when that happens, so I try to make sure it doesn't."

"How do you prevent it?" Tracy asked.

"For one thing, everyone has to show a photo ID when they make a transaction," Mitch said. "We keep track of who brings in what. I record serial numbers for items that have them, in case I have to submit that to the police. Mostly I use my gut. If someone comes in every other week with a new laptop or a collection of jewelry to pawn, I'm reasonably sure they're not on the up-and-up. If someone is crying about parting with their mother's necklace, I tend to believe it's theirs."

Tracy mulled over the information. "You said you hold items in another room until the owner returns for them—or not. So if someone brought you something in the past day or so, it wouldn't be out here, but in there, right?"

"That's right, if they were going to pawn it. But I can tell you no one has pawned any kind of computer recently. We do have a laptop and a few phones people sold us though. I'll show you."

Mitch showed her a sleek black laptop, but it wasn't the brand that either she or Jeff owned.

"That's not it," she said. "What about the phones?"

"Right here." He gestured toward the shelf where half a dozen phones sat. She wasn't sure what Anna's phone looked like, but she didn't recognize the sleek white-and-gold case she knew Anna used. She also didn't see a ring light.

"You can come to the back room," Mitch said. "You can let me know if we have any of your other items there."

"You'd let me do that?"

"I don't want stolen goods in my shop," Mitch said. "If we have them, we'll let the police know right away. Why don't you give me a description of the items you're looking for?"

Tracy rattled off a list of the stolen items and described each one as thoroughly as she could. Afterwards, he led her to a room about half the size of the main one, filled with a similar array of items. She headed first to the shelves of laptops and scanned them, hunting for hers and Jeff's. She spotted a few of the same brand. But none were the right color or shape, so she wandered over to the glass case where jewelry was laid out on a red background. There was nothing like the ruby ring in Lincoln's picture, and no diamond earrings at all.

"I don't see them," Tracy said.

"I'll keep an eye out for them," Mitch said. "If someone does bring in items matching your description, I'll be sure to let the police know right away."

"Could you also let me know?" Tracy asked. She reached into her purse, took out her notebook, and tore a page from it. She wrote down her email address and handed the paper to Mitch.

"Sure," he said.

"Thank you." Tracy walked back out to her car, unsettled. She was grateful she'd never had to use the services of a pawn shop before, and hoped she never would, though she found herself newly aware of the need in her community.

She returned to the office, where she wrote and submitted her sanitation department story. She also finished her column about Tully and sent it in, and then she slung her purse over her shoulder and headed out again.

Tracy thought about visiting the pawn shops in Quincy to see if they had the missing items, but she decided that could wait. Instead, she would pay a visit to Jody Bonilla, whose name kept coming up as someone who had behaved oddly the night of the party. It wouldn't be weird to take Jody some cookies and welcome her to the church. After all, Pastor Gary had encouraged the members to follow up after the progressive dinner to make sure the newcomers felt loved.

She could take Amy along, since she had been in the same group as Jody and had spent more time with her that night. The dinner was all about getting to know new members, after all, and getting them settled at the church. And if Tracy managed to learn a bit more about Jody's actions that night at the same time—well, that would be a bonus.

Jody had told them at the dinner where she lived. She said she'd moved into the big pink Victorian a couple blocks away from Tracy. Tracy knew it because of the color, the patches of fish-scale siding, and the stained glass window over the door, which Tracy had always admired. So finding Jody wasn't the problem. The issue was that Tracy, a Midwesterner through and through, did not want to show up at her place empty-handed. Fortunately, that problem was easily solved with a quick trip to Buttermilk Bakeshop.

On the way back downtown, Tracy called Amy. School had let out, so she guessed Amy would be packing up to leave.

"Hey, Tracy," her sister sang out. "What's up?"

"I was wondering if you had time to come with me to visit Jody Bonilla."

"Is this a social visit, or are you sleuthing?"

"Both?"

Amy laughed. "Sounds great. When?"

"I was thinking this afternoon, if you're around."

"I'm just finishing up here. The kids have their after-school running club today, so I have forty-five minutes until I need to be back to pick them up. Do you want to swing by here in the next ten minutes or so?"

"That sounds perfect." That would give her enough time to stop in at the bakery and make it to the school.

A few minutes later, Tracy parked in front of the bakery. Inside, a long marble counter was piled with trays of croissants and muffins and bagels and tarts. Tables were scattered throughout the open dining area, several of them occupied by small groups of people enjoying coffee and pastries while they chatted. Daphne, a shop assistant Tracy had met before, was at the register, and owner Mariella was bringing out a tray of freshly baked cookies.

"Hello, Tracy." Mariella smiled. Her dark hair was pulled back into a ponytail under a paper hat. "Are you okay? I heard about what happened on Saturday." She set the tray on the marble counter.

"I'm all right," Tracy said. "Though I'm sure hoping the stolen items get recovered."

"Me too," Mariella said. "It must feel like such a violation, to have someone you invited into your home do something like that." She picked up a thin metal spatula to transfer chocolate chip cookies from the tray to a display stand on the marble counter.

"That's it exactly," Tracy said. "You didn't happen to see anything out of the ordinary during the evening, did you?"

Mariella had been in the second group. She'd spent the evening with Paula, Sharon and Caleb, and Kevin and Sara as well as their kids.

"I've been going over the evening, trying to remember." Mariella placed another cookie on the stand. It was plump and studded with chunks of chocolate, and the center had a slight depression, signaling gooey goodness inside. "I don't think I saw anything strange, to be honest. The most likely possibility in our group—and I feel terrible even thinking this—is Caleb, Sharon's son. He had a big backpack with him. It was kind of odd, honestly, because what does a teenage boy need to carry around during a party?"

"I remember that," Tracy said. "It was a black backpack, right?" She hadn't thought anything of it at the time, because nearly all the attendees had carried bags or purses, but most everyone else drove, so they needed their wallet and keys, at the very least. Mariella brought up a good point. What had Caleb needed a big backpack for?

"That's right," Mariella said. "And he brought it into the house with him each time instead of leaving it in the car."

"Maybe it had something valuable inside," Tracy suggested. "One of those handheld video games, maybe? Just in case he could slip away from the adults for a few minutes?"

"Maybe," Mariella said, but Tracy could see she was skeptical about that idea.

"We'll see what the police find," Tracy said, though she was about to do some reconnaissance of her own. "In the meantime, would you box up half a dozen of those cookies for me? They smell too tempting to resist."

"Coming right up." Mariella put the cookies into a white bakery box and tied it with a red-and-white string. "I'll be praying that the truth comes to light quickly."

"Thank you." Tracy paid for the cookies, carried the box to her car, and made the short drive to the elementary school.

Amy waited for her on the sidewalk in front. She hopped into the car and buckled her seat belt. "So, what's our strategy?"

"I think we should talk about how much we enjoyed meeting her and make some normal small talk," Tracy said. "And then casually mention the missing items and see how she responds."

"But also peek around and see if we notice a few extra laptops or diamonds, right?" Amy said, grinning.

"Obviously, though if she leaves stolen items lying around in plain sight in her home, she's not the most savvy thief."

"I'll be on the lookout anyway."

Tracy parked on the street, noting the BMW in the driveway. "Someone's home." She gathered her purse and the box of cookies, and together they made their way to the sidewalk. The paint on the front of the house was flaking, and a gutter needed to be repaired, but the house was still beautiful, painted in shades of pink. Tracy loved the way the soft colors accentuated the home's ornate, cream-colored trim.

Tracy walked up the porch steps and knocked on the door. After a moment, Jody opened it.

"Hello, Tracy. Hi, Amy." A wide smile spread across Jody's face. The single mom was in her late thirties, if Tracy had to guess, and her brown hair had honey-colored highlights framing her face. She wore form-fitting jeans, a sweater printed with tan, red, and black plaid lines, and large diamond stud earrings. "It's good to see you again."

Tracy held out the box. "We wanted to stop by and welcome you to the Faith Church community."

"You two are the sweetest. Please, come on in." She took the box and stepped back so they could follow her inside. "We're still unpacking, so it's kind of a mess."

She ushered them into what would have once been a formal front parlor but now was filled with modern furniture. An oversize sectional in deep gray velvet dominated the room, flanked by armchairs in light-colored leather. A marble coffee table sat in front of them.

Cardboard boxes were piled in the corner. They didn't appear to be moving boxes but rather shipping boxes. Tracy recognized the logos of three different online retailers. The furniture wasn't to her taste, but the room was nice enough. She didn't see any laptops or phones.

"Please, have a seat." Jody gestured at the couch. Music thumped upstairs. Tracy remembered Jody had a teenage daughter. "Can I get you some coffee? Tea?"

"No thank you." Tracy thought quickly, anxious to see more of the house. "This is such a beautiful home. I've always wondered about it, but I've never been inside. It's every bit as gorgeous outside as it is inside."

"Thank you," Jody said. "As soon as I saw it, I knew I had to live here. I love old homes, and this one has so many original details left." She gestured at a carved lattice screen over the doorway.

"Is that a formal dining room in there?" Tracy started down the hallway. Jody hadn't invited her to tour the house, but anyone who loved their house like Jody did would be glad to show it off.

"Yes," Jody said, coming up behind her. "I've always wanted one. Back in St. Louis, we lived in a typical suburban home. We didn't have anything like this. I can't wait to host holidays here."

Tracy stepped into the room, which was dominated by a long wooden table surrounded by tufted green chairs. A wood and steel chandelier hung over the table. More boxes from online retailers were on the table—high-end retailers, from the names Tracy recognized.

"This is lovely," Tracy said. There were plenty of boxes, but if one of them contained the stolen items, she couldn't see it.

"And this kitchen," Amy enthused, following Tracy's lead and continuing down the hallway. "This is gorgeous."

When Tracy stepped into the kitchen, she saw that it was done in a French country style, with off-white cabinets, soapstone counters, and a pot rack with copper pots over the six-burner professional range. The refrigerator was huge and was a brand Tracy had never heard of, but she could tell it wasn't cheap. There were also two ovens with red knobs, a microwave under the counter, a pot-filler faucet over the stove, and a beverage fridge.

"Thank you," Jody said, setting the box of cookies on the counter. "I had it upgraded before we moved in."

"I really like it," Tracy said. It truly was nice. Tracy loved her own kitchen, but Jody's had luxury touches she could only dream about. Still, no laptops, no jewels, no extra phones.

"Are you going to paint the outside?" Amy asked.

"No." Jody shook her head. "I love living in a pink house. My ex would never have been okay with that, so I enjoy it all the more."

"When do you start your job at the college?" Tracy asked. Jody had mentioned on Saturday that she'd moved to Canton to take a job in development at Culver-Stockton College. Jeff had worked there in the history department long enough for Tracy to understand that meant Jody would be fundraising. Given the state of her home, Tracy imagined she would be pretty good at it.

"Next week," Jody said. "I'm excited to get going."

"How do you like Canton so far?" Tracy asked. "It's quite different from St. Louis."

"I've always wanted to live in a small town," Jody said. "My ex didn't want to, but I don't have to worry about him anymore."

Tracy didn't know how to respond to that, but Amy said, "Your split was pretty recent, wasn't it?"

"Yes." Jody toyed with a ring on her right hand, a matte silver swirl of a thing. "It's only been about six months."

"I'm sorry," Tracy said.

"We're doing all right," Jody said. "We've got this great house, a new job, a whole new start."

But something about her tone rang false, as if she was trying too hard to make it true. Was she trying to convince them, or herself?

And what, exactly, did she want to convince them of?

Chapter Seven

Tracy didn't even realize she'd let the conversation lapse while she mused until Amy broke the silence. "How does your daughter like it in Canton, Jody? Is she adjusting?"

"It's a big change," Jody said. "But kids are tough, and Louisa will get there."

"It's a lot all at once," Amy said. "Her parents' divorce, a new town, a new school."

"It is. I keep telling her to give it a chance." The smile on Jody's face didn't quite reach her eyes. "I tried to get her to come with me on Saturday to meet some new people, but she preferred to stay home. All in good time, I suppose."

"Maybe she should check out the youth group," Tracy said. "My kids always enjoyed it."

"I'm sure she'll find her way." Again, Jody's smile seemed a little too forced to be convincing. "And everyone here has been so welcoming."

"I'm so glad you feel that way. It's a wonderful church," Tracy said.

"Though something strange did happen on Saturday night," Amy said, jumping in as Tracy had hoped she would. "I'm sure you've heard about that."

"At the progressive dinner?" Jody asked, eyes wide.

"Yes. Things were taken from some of the hosts' houses," Amy said.

"Really?" Jody's mouth dropped open.

Was Jody genuinely surprised? Tracy didn't see how she could be. Even if she hadn't heard about the thefts—or committed them herself—the police were interviewing everyone, weren't they?

"Yes," Tracy said. "My laptop was taken, as was my husband's."

"Jeff's was taken? He told me it was brand-new."

"It was," Tracy said.

"I'm so sorry," Jody said. "That was a nice machine."

"Well, we're hoping the police will recover it," Tracy said. "It was more than the laptops though. My daughter-in-law's phone was taken, along with a ring light. Some of Melody Bailey's jewelry was stolen, and Paula Jordan is missing her phone as well."

"Oh my goodness. This all happened during the event?" Jody was either truly surprised or she was a very good actress.

"That's right," Tracy said. "The police are investigating. They're talking to everyone who was there that night. Haven't they been here to speak with you?"

Jody shook her head. "Would they have come by, or called?"

"I think they're visiting everybody in person," Tracy said. "But I really don't know."

"Well, if they've been here, Louisa and I must not have been home." Jody pulled a phone from her pocket and looked at the screen. Tracy noticed it was a newer model. "Oh, wait, there's a message here." She touched the screen and put the phone to her ear. After a moment she clicked it off. "That was Dale Leewright. He wants me to call him." She checked the phone again. "That came in yesterday, and I totally missed it. I'm so sorry. I'll call him back, but I don't have anything useful to tell him, I'm afraid."

"You didn't see anything out of the ordinary?" Amy asked. "We wondered if you might have while you were out of the room at some point, either at Tracy's or at one of the other places."

"I don't think so." Jody set the phone on the counter.

"You did leave the table to use the restroom, and you were gone for quite a while," Tracy said. She continued quickly, so Jody wouldn't think she was accusing her. "We wondered if you might have heard or seen anything strange during that time."

"No." Jody shook her head. "Did anyone else leave the dining room while I was gone?"

"Jeff made some trips to the kitchen," Tracy said. She didn't want to push too hard, but she also didn't want to ignore the opportunity to find out what Jody would say. "You were gone so long that we actually wondered if everything was okay."

"Oh. Yes." Jody pressed her lips together, and then she sighed. "I'm sorry. I wondered about that, honestly. I had hoped you all didn't notice how long I was gone." She didn't appear embarrassed, as Tracy would have expected. In fact, *defeated* was the word that came to Tracy.

Amy started to say, "You don't have to tell us—"

Tracy cut her off. "Was everything all right?"

Jody sighed again. "It was Louisa, actually. She was in such a state. We got into a fight right before the dinner, if you want to know the truth. I wanted her to come with me, and she refused, and—well, it was difficult. I ended up leaving her here, because what can you do, right? It's not like when she was little and I could carry her to the car." Jody laughed, a hollow, brittle sound.

"Was she okay?" Amy asked.

"She'll be fine," Jody said. "Like I said, she'll adjust. But like you said, she's going through a lot of changes all at once. She's hurt and angry about the divorce, about the move, about leaving her friends behind. She's worried she won't meet anyone she likes. I can't fix it for her, and she doesn't want me to. She blames me. You know the drill."

Tracy finally felt that Jody was being real with them for the first time, as if her carefully constructed mask had been knocked askew and allowed them a glimpse of the truth.

"Parenting teenagers is hard even in the best situation," she said. "In these circumstances, it has to be brutal, and you're suddenly doing it alone."

Tears shimmered in Jody's eyes. "Anyway, there was a lot of door-slamming and some shouting. I'm ashamed to admit it, but the fight continued over text throughout the night. It was not one of my best parenting moments. When I went to use the bathroom at your place, I went in there to talk to Louisa. It happened at the other houses too."

Tracy really did empathize. Chad and Sara had been good kids, but they still managed to drive her and Jeff crazy during their teenage years. A surly teen dealing with her parents' divorce and a life she hadn't asked to be thrust into could be a whole other ball game. "I'm so sorry to hear it," Tracy said. "Is everything okay now?"

Jody gestured upward. "I haven't heard much besides the music for the past few days. She emerges when she's hungry, but she doesn't speak to me."

"Sometimes these things take a while to blow over," Tracy said.

"In any case, I'm afraid I really don't know anything about the missing items, but I'll call the police and cooperate however I can," Jody said.

"Thank you," Tracy said. She tried to think of an elegant way to ask her next question—about how Jody as a single mother with a job at a small college could afford so many nice things—but the best she could come up with was, "By the way, those are beautiful earrings."

Jody touched her ears gently, as if trying to remind herself what she had on. "Thank you. They were a gift from my ex, and as much as that makes me want to get rid of them, I love them too much."

"I can see why. They're gorgeous."

They chatted for a few more minutes about Jody's plans to continue updating the house, and then Amy announced she had to go pick up her kids, so they made their way to the door.

Jody hugged them. "Thank you so much for coming by. It means a lot to see how this church has reached out and embraced us."

"We're so glad you're here." Tracy and Amy waved as they made their way to the car. Tracy mentally crossed Jody off the suspect list as they walked.

As soon as they were buckled in, she said, "So what did you think?"

"I was extremely interested in the brand names everywhere. She definitely has a shopping habit."

"I did notice she'd ordered a lot of things, but she is starting over in life."

"Yeah, but that was a high-quality sweater. Cashmere, if I'm not mistaken. In fact, I recognized most of the high-end brands I saw in there, from her fancy coffee maker to the professional-grade appliances in the kitchen."

"How did you recognize those?"

"We've been looking at updating our kitchen, so I've been researching stoves. I immediately ruled out one like hers because it was way out of our price range. The coffee maker has been in ads all over the place. It's the next big thing. Haven't you seen it?"

"I haven't," Tracy said.

Amy gave a deep sigh. "You're hopeless."

"I did see a BMW," Tracy protested.

"Yes, and that proves my point. She likes designer brands. Flashy ones, at that. She's not going for understated. She likes brands people will recognize."

Tracy rounded a corner. "If she likes them and can afford them, I guess it's up to her how she spends her money."

"Very true. I'm just not sure how a newly single mom with an assistant fundraising job at a small college can afford them."

"Maybe she has family money. Or her ex is loaded and she got a great alimony deal on top of child support."

"All possibilities," Amy agreed. "But I also saw a past-due notice on the table in the kitchen. It was from her credit card company."

"How did you see that?"

"It was right out in the open. Honestly, you're supposed to be the observant one." Amy grinned. "Anyway, I saw that as well as all the brand names. It's almost as if she's anxious to project an image, and that image is that she's doing great."

"For all we know, she is." But Tracy knew it sounded weak. Jody was not doing great, or she wouldn't have spent half of Saturday night in the bathroom arguing with her teenage daughter. "Anyway, well-spotted, but did you see any laptops or phones or a ring light with those eagle eyes of yours?"

"Phones? As in, plural?"

"Yeah. Paula Jordan's phone also vanished that night."

"Great. No, I didn't see any of them," Amy said, "but that doesn't mean she doesn't have them. I did see the diamond earrings she had on, which could be the ones Melody lost. Nice job asking about those."

"Except they were a gift from her ex," Tracy said.

"Were they?" Amy raised an eyebrow.

"She said they were," Tracy insisted.

"And she may be telling the truth, but I don't want to eliminate the possibility that she wasn't, given that they matched the description of a stolen item."

"Fair enough." Tracy pulled into the lot in front of the elementary school. "Well, I think she's at the bottom of the suspect list at this point."

"As long as she's still on it, and I think she needs to be," Amy said.

"I'll agree to that," Tracy said. "Thanks for coming."

"Anytime. I've always wanted to see inside that house." Amy hopped out and closed the door then waved and strode toward the school.

Tracy checked the time. She should probably head home and get dinner started. But after her comment to Amy about Paula, she realized she had spoken to almost everyone who had items taken—except Paula. She decided to make one more stop before she headed home.

Tracy parked outside Huckleberry Books a few minutes later. Jeannie Morrison lived above the bookshop with her kids. Her mother had moved in a few years back after Jeannie's divorce. Tracy could see Jeannie straightening books on the front table, so she decided to stop there first.

"Hi, Tracy," Jeannie said, stepping away from a stack of cookbooks. "How are you?"

"I'm good," Tracy said. She took a deep breath, inhaling the soothing aroma of paper and ink. Bookstores smelled like heaven. She scanned the shop, which was filled with light from the big picture window at the front. Pastel-colored shelves lined the shop floor, and a few people read in the velvet armchairs by the fireplace.

"Any word on the thefts?" Jeannie asked.

"Not yet," Tracy said. "How about your mom? Has she gotten any word on her phone?"

Jeannie shook her head, and her honey-blond hair brushed against her shoulders. "No."

"I was actually hoping to speak with her about that," Tracy said. "Is she around?"

"She's upstairs with the kids. I'm sure she'd be happy to talk to you," Jeannie said. "Why don't you go on up? I'll give her a call on the landline and let her know you're coming."

"Thank you." Tracy took one last longing glance at the books before she made her way up the stairs that led to the second floor.

By the time she made it to the landing, Paula had the door open and was smiling at her. Her white hair was cut into a neat bob, and her glasses hung on a chain around her neck. She wore a long, loose cardigan over a black turtleneck and dark slacks. "Tracy. It's good to see you again."

"You too."

"Have you found the thief yet?" Paula asked.

"The police are still investigating." Tracy entered the apartment. It had high ceilings and big windows that let in lots of light. A large living room was directly in front of her, and Jeannie's kids, Kira and Max, were seated on a big brown couch, watching a show.

Paula raised an eyebrow at her as she closed the door. "I didn't ask what *they* were doing. You're good at solving mysteries, so I thought you might figure this out before they do."

Tracy laughed. "Well, I can tell you I've been asking some questions, but I haven't figured anything out yet. I was hoping to find out more about your phone."

"Sure. The police were here yesterday, but I was wondering when you'd drop by. Come on. We can sit here." Paula indicated a table on the other side of the apartment, next to an open kitchen with white cabinets and a granite counter. "Tea?"

"Yes, please."

Tracy sat down and selected a mint tea from the basket on the table while Paula heated water in an electric kettle. When the water was hot, she poured it over the tea bag.

Tracy wrapped her hands around the warm mug. "I wondered if you could tell me when you last saw your phone," she said. "Did you use it anytime during the evening Saturday?"

"Yes," Paula said. "I had it when I drove to Pastor Gary's house, because I used it to navigate there. I put it in my bag before I went into the house. Someone must have stolen it while we were eating brownies at his place."

"It was taken at Pastor Gary's?" Was that why nothing that belonged to the Bennetts had been taken? Because the thief had stolen Paula's phone there instead? "Are you sure you didn't leave it in the car?"

"I'm sure." Paula dunked her bag of chamomile in the hot water in her mug. "Jeannie looked through the car for me this morning, and it's not there."

"When did you discover it was missing?"

"Not until the next day," Paula said, shaking her head. "When I went to call my son after church to check in, like I do every Sunday. He lives in Colorado, so I don't get to see him much. But when I went to call him, the phone was gone."

"Where do you normally keep it?" Tracy asked.

"Jeannie tells me to keep it by the door so I always know where it is and I can grab it when I go out, but the truth is that it usually ends up at the bottom of my bag most days. That's why I didn't notice it was gone for so long."

"Do you always use the same bag?" Tracy blew on her tea then took a sip. It was hot, and the mint flavor wonderfully soothing.

"I gave up cute purses a few years ago, after I had surgery on my shoulder. Now I always use a backpack. It's over there." She gestured toward the door, where a small black backpack sat on a low bench, next to a coatrack that was surrounded by a collection of shoes. "You can go through it if you want, but the phone's not there."

"I believe you," Tracy said. Jeannie would have searched thoroughly, so even if Paula had somehow missed it, Jeannie would have found it. "What kind of phone was it?"

"An older one," Paula said. "In a blue rubber case. I've had it for quite a while. It was all scratched up and dinged. Jeannie was always on me to get a new one, but nothing's wrong with the one I had."

That didn't sound quite as valuable as the other items that were taken Saturday night. But a cell phone was still a cell phone, which meant it was still likely to bring some profit, even if it wasn't much.

"Does your phone have a feature that lets you see where it is? Like a Locate app?"

"Jeannie tells me it does and that I should have registered my phone for it, but I had never heard of it until yesterday."

"Did you see anyone acting strangely, or anything that would give you any idea about who might have taken it?" Tracy drained her cup.

"Unfortunately, no," Paula said. "I can't understand it. It still doesn't make sense."

Out of both tea and helpful questions, Tracy stood to leave. "Thank you for your help."

"Thank *you*," Paula said. "I sure hope you find it. Not just my phone, but all the stuff that was taken."

"I do too." Tracy waved goodbye to Max and Kira then headed back down the stairs and out to her car.

As she drove home, Tracy mulled over the theft of Paula's phone. Something about it struck her as different from the other thefts. For one, it wasn't taken from a host, and for another, it wasn't something new or valuable. But there was no denying that it had happened and that Paula deserved answers just as much as anyone.

Chapter Eight

When Tracy got home, she found Robin's car in the driveway and her purse on the table. Tom's and Angie's jackets hung on the coatrack, next to Robin's. She checked her phone. She'd missed Robin's text that they were on their way over.

"Hello?" she called. There was no answer. They must be in the attic.

Tracy set her things down and went up the stairs to the second floor. The pull-down ladder was already in place, and the hatch lay open. She scaled the rungs and found Robin and Tom hunched over a steamer trunk. Angie thumbed through books on a shelf in another part of the attic. Sunlight streamed in through the windows, helping the lone light bulb that struggled to light the room. The old stained glass rose window cast colorful beams along a set of bookcases.

"Hey." Tracy threaded her way toward them between piles of boxes. "Any luck?"

Tom and Robin raised their heads, and Tracy noticed how alike they were. They shared the same dark brown hair and heart-shaped face.

Angie smiled a greeting then went back to the books.

"Not yet," Tom said. "Though we found a bunch of Grandpa's things from the forties, so we're hoping there's something mixed in with all that."

"Oh wow." Tracy saw that they had found Grandpa Howard's dress uniform from the navy, double-breasted and deep blue with brass buttons.

"We found this too," Robin said, holding out a small box lined with velvet. A medal rested gently on its surface.

Tracy gasped. "Is that his Purple Heart?" He'd received one after a bullet fractured his leg when he rescued a fellow sailor.

"It is," Robin said, holding it out.

Tracy took it reverently. She couldn't imagine having the kind of courage Grandpa had shown that day.

"And we found these old papers from his job back then," Tom said. Grandpa Howard had worked in an ammunition factory in St. Louis after his honorable discharge, coming home on weekends to see Grandma. "Pay stubs, personnel records—all kinds of things."

"And this was tucked in with some souvenirs from their wedding," Robin said, holding up a framed formal portrait of their grandparents posed in front of Faith Church. Grandpa wore a dark suit, the jacket long and slim, with a tie and pocket square. Grandma wore a long-sleeved white silk dress cinched at the waist, along with a long veil over her rolled hair. Why was the photo tucked away in a chest up here, instead of on display in the house? Tracy set it aside to take downstairs with her.

"The watch was a gift from the man he saved in battle, right?" Tracy asked. Family lore said that the man had returned from the war and started a furniture company and had never forgotten that Grandpa was the reason he'd made it out alive. They'd reunited many years after that fateful day, and he had given Grandpa the Rolex as a token of gratitude.

"That's what we believe." Robin hoisted a stack of papers out of the trunk and set them on a nearby table. "Why didn't anyone ever buy Grandpa a filing cabinet?"

"He had one," Tracy said with a chuckle. "We found it up here one time, still in its box. He never got around to using it."

Tom reached into the trunk again and pulled out a collection of neckties in varying shades of blue and red, and Tracy found a collection of coins from around the world in a plastic baggie. She wondered if any of them were valuable but decided now wasn't the time to sort through them. She set the coins aside as Robin cried, "Aha!"

"What did you find?" Tracy asked.

Robin held up a few papers and a small booklet paper-clipped together. *Rolex* was written on the front of the booklet. Robin took off the clip and looked through the papers. "Here's a receipt from Famous-Barr in St. Louis. And this is information about the watch. It says it's a 1955 Rolex Datejust."

"That's right," Tom said. "That's the model."

Robin flipped through the pages, and a folded piece of paper fell out. Tracy picked it up, unfolded it, and skimmed the small writing quickly. "This certifies that Grandpa Howard's watch was a genuine Rolex," she told the others.

"So now we need to figure out when it was switched," Tom said.

"And where the real one is now," Robin added. "I don't think I ever looked at it that closely before I met the dealer who taught me about watches, so I'm afraid I can't narrow down the time frame."

Tracy tried to phrase her next idea carefully. "Grandpa loved that watch. He took such pride in it, and I bet he would have noticed if something had happened to it. But after he passed, it went to Dad."

Tom and Robin nodded.

"Your dad also loved the watch," Robin said.

"He did, but for different reasons," Tracy said. "Grandpa was proud of what it represented, and there was a certain status in owning a Rolex. But I don't think Dad really knew the difference. I think he liked the watch because it had belonged to his father."

"Are you saying Grandpa would have noticed if his watch suddenly wasn't a Rolex, but Uncle Noah wouldn't have?" Tom asked.

"I'm merely trying to come up with possibilities," she said. "My dad was a bit scatterbrained."

"So someone got their hands on a replica of the watch, waited for the right opportunity when Uncle Noah wasn't wearing it, and switched it out?" Tom asked. "That seems really unlikely."

"It does when you put it that way," Robin acknowledged.

"Or it could have happened after I inherited it," Tom said, his tone reluctant. "I love the watch too, but I don't know enough about Rolexes to have picked up on the details Robin noticed." He grimaced. "Clearly."

"Why did it go to you and not to Chad?" Robin asked.

"It probably should have," Tom said, "but he was three at the time, so Grandma thought it made more sense for me to take it."

"That's what my dad would have wanted," Tracy said. "My dad was Grandpa's only son, and you're the only grandson. It made sense for it to end up with you."

"I've had it since 1997, when Uncle Noah passed," Tom said. "I suppose it could have been swapped out any time since then."

Angie left the bookshelf and joined them. "It wouldn't have been easy. You wear it a lot."

Tracy paper-clipped the papers and booklet back together. "Do you remember anyone asking to see it, or taking it off to show someone?"

"I don't," Tom said. "But seriously, 1997. That's twenty-seven years ago. I guess I could have done that sometime, especially when I first got it."

"Where do you put it when you're not wearing it?" Tracy asked.

Tom ducked his head. "I'm not as careful about that as I should be," he admitted. "I just put it wherever I happen to take it off. On an end table, on the kitchen counter, on my nightstand."

"That's true," Angie said. "I'm always telling him to put it somewhere safe where it won't get spilled on or knocked off."

"So it could have been lying around waiting for someone to take it," Robin said. "Do you remember anyone who showed interest in it or who might have wanted it?"

"I mean, it's a Rolex. Lots of people could have wanted it." Tom shrugged.

"What about Larry?" Angie asked. "Didn't you say he noticed the watch?"

"Yeah, but he's a good guy. He wouldn't have taken it."

"Who's Larry?" Tracy asked.

"He's a contractor who's been doing some work on our house," Angie explained.

"I didn't know about that," Robin said.

"It's nothing major. We're fixing a few things we should have fixed long ago," Tom said. "Larry's been around a lot the past few weeks, and he did notice my watch when I met him. But that doesn't mean he took it." He shrugged again. "And I didn't take it off to show it to him."

"Was there ever a time when Larry was alone in the house with the watch?" Angie asked.

"Probably," Tom said. "But I'll say it again. That doesn't mean he took it."

"You're right," Robin said soothingly. "It doesn't mean that. We're going over possibilities, not accusing anyone."

"Okay, so what are the other possibilities?" Tracy asked. "Have you had it serviced recently? Or repaired?"

"Not recently," Tom said. "The last time was when I took it to the jeweler here in Canton because I wanted to use the same place Grandpa and Uncle Noah used. It was a year ago Christmas, and I brought it to them to replace the battery and make sure it was running right. I think they had it for a night or two. But you can't seriously think a jeweler would have swapped out my Rolex for a fake."

"It doesn't seem like a jeweler who did something like that would be in business for very long," Tracy acknowledged.

"And Dimas Jewelers has been around for decades," Robin said. "Simon Dimas is a good guy."

"But it must have been the Rolex when Tom took it in," Tracy said. "Simon would have known if it was a fake and would've said something."

"You're right," Robin said. "Okay, so we've narrowed down our timeline significantly. We know Tom had Grandpa's watch sixteen months ago. It must have been switched out since then. Which means it's not looking great for that contractor."

Tom nodded reluctantly.

"I think it's worth a visit to Dimas Jewelers to confirm that Simon saw the real Rolex when he serviced it," Tracy suggested.

"And it's probably worth checking with that contractor to see what he can tell you about the last time he saw your watch," Robin said.

Tom sighed but didn't argue. "I do want to find Grandpa's watch. Let me see what I can find out."

Chapter Nine

When Tracy walked into work Tuesday morning, she meant to focus on editing her story and finishing her column, yet the first thing she did was open up the auction site again. She would have done so at home, but it would have been annoying to use her phone's tiny screen and keyboard for such research.

She powered up her computer, made herself a cup of coffee, and searched the auction site for any new laptops listed in the area that matched the description of their missing computers. There were a few possibilities, but it was so hard to tell.

"Hey, Tracy."

Tracy whipped around. She'd been so absorbed she hadn't heard anyone walk up behind her.

"Sorry to startle you. I wondered if you'd had any news on the thefts," Bethany said. Her hair was in a messy bun, and she wore a white T-shirt with pants printed in a jungle design.

"Sadly, no," Tracy said. "I tried to find the missing laptops on this auction site, but I'm not having much luck."

"Have you checked out Resell-IT?"

"What?"

"Resell-IT. Like 'resell it,' but also like 'IT,' as in information technology."

"I've never heard of it."

"It's a good site for finding used tech. I've bought and sold a few things on there. The prices are good, and it's easy to use. Here, let me show you."

"Be my guest." Tracy scooted over to make room.

Bethany pulled up a chair and opened a new tab then typed away, logging on to her account on the site. WELCOME, CIRCUITQUEEN13 appeared at the top right of the screen, and then Bethany selected a tab that said BUY.

"What kind of laptop was it?" she asked.

After her fruitless search with too little information the day before, Tracy had taken the time to hunt down the paperwork for her laptop. She told Bethany the model name and year, and Bethany typed them in.

"There are a dozen or so available," she said. "You can click on each one and try to figure out if it's yours."

Tracy selected the first photo and studied it. Then she clicked on the next one. They looked just the same. How was she supposed to know if it was hers or not? And all the items appeared to be for sale by the site rather than individual sellers.

"Is the site itself selling these items?"

"Yeah, that's how this one works," Bethany said. "People sell their stuff to the site, and then the site resells it."

"Why is it so cheap?" These machines were about half the price of the ones she'd seen listed online.

Bethany hesitated. When she answered, it sounded as if she chose her words carefully. "Most people on traditional auction sites are willing to hold on to their item if it doesn't sell at the price they want. This site is more for people who need cash now. So people sell their items directly to the site at a lower price than they could get elsewhere, but they get the money right away. It's a good place to get electronics without spending a lot of money."

It also sounded like an easy way to sell stolen electronics, Tracy thought.

Tracy clicked around, hunting for anything that resembled the missing items. It was so hard to tell, especially since there was no way to know where the items originally came from. "Thanks for helping me with this, Bethany."

"I don't know if you'll find anything, but it's worth checking out," Bethany said, shrugging. "Anyway, looks like you've got work to do."

Tracy raised her head to see Annette coming toward her, papers in hand, so Bethany patted her shoulder, smiled at Jake—who had arrived during their conversation—and headed back to her desk.

Annette chatted for a few minutes about her new grandbaby, who had been born around the same time as Chad and Anna's youngest. The discussion moved on to the edits needed on Tracy's articles. When Annette left, Tracy went to work making the necessary changes. After she sent them in, she proofed some copy and sorted through her inbox.

Shortly before noon, Tracy had cleared her to-do list, so she went back to the site Bethany had shown her and clicked around, but she didn't come up with much. It was certainly possible that some of the items for sale were their stolen electronics, but there was no way to tell for sure. Tracy should be out and about, talking to the suspects, checking pawn shops, and generally doing something more productive than investigating a website that was starting to feel like a dead end.

She had spoken to one of the suspects already that morning. Though if Bethany was the thief, why would she show Tracy the auction site she frequented? Then again, maybe she had done so to distract her from another site where she had actually sold the stolen items.

Tracy's phone rang, and she was glad to see that Robin was calling her. She needed a distraction. She swiped her screen. "Hey, Robin."

"Hi, Tracy. I'm going over to Dimas Jewelers, and I wondered if you wanted to come with me."

"Ooh, are we going shopping?" Tracy joked.

Robin laughed. "You feel free to buy yourself something shiny. I'm going to ask about Tom's watch, and I thought it might help if you were there too. I've used Simon for years to repair pieces for the shop, and I trust him completely, which is why I need you."

"Because I don't trust him?"

"Because you'll question things I won't."

Tracy had to admit that was probably true. "When are you planning to go?"

"Millie should be here in about an hour. Would leaving then work for you?"

"That should be fine," Tracy said. She would check with Annette about any final edits, and she should have time to eat lunch as well. "I'll meet you at the shop then."

Tracy ate the chicken salad sandwich she'd brought for lunch while she made the finishing touches to her article. Then she grabbed her purse and made the short walk to Pearls of Wisdom.

She found Robin inside, dusting a bulbous silver lamp that had dragons coming out of the sides and a round glass shade.

"That's quite a lamp," Tracy said.

"It's a Bradley and Hubbard from 1923," Robin said. "It was originally an oil lamp, but it's been electrified. It's really rare."

"In that case, I hope you sell it for big bucks."

"Me too." Robin grinned and called, "We're headed out, Millie."

"I've got it." Millie waved from behind the counter. "Have fun."

Tracy and Robin walked the two blocks to Dimas Jewelers, a narrow little shop that had opened in 1944, according to its sign. Tracy knew that many an engagement ring in her family had been purchased there, including Robin's, Anna's, and her own. Simon Dimas had inherited the shop from his father. He was a fixture in town, and he knew his jewels. There was a newer chain store in the mall, but they had nothing on his little shop.

Inside, glass cases were set in a U-shape, and a little door at the bottom of the U led to the small office and workroom at the back. The walls were old-school wood paneling, and the thin industrial carpet was stained an indefinite dark color. The black velvet that lined the cases had been bleached by the sun. The place hadn't been updated in decades.

But none of that mattered next to the breathtaking jewelry. Tracy stepped up to the first display case, which showcased necklaces with all kinds of stones—amethysts, sapphires, garnets, diamonds, and more that she didn't recognize. She moved to the next case, which held earrings. A set of opal earrings, which showed sparks of different colors as she moved, caught her eye.

"Good afternoon." The tall young woman who came from the workroom had curly dark hair that hung to her shoulders, and her fair skin made her blue eyes stand out. She wore a floral-print top and a gold rose pendant on a matching chain. On her left hand was a diamond ring that rivaled anything in the shop. Tracy didn't know much about jewels, but she would have guessed the stone was at least two carats, maybe more. "Can I help you with something?"

"We were hoping to talk to Simon," Robin said, nodding toward the office. "Is he around?"

"Sure thing." She walked to the doorway and called, "Uncle Simon, there are people here to talk to you." She must have heard a response, because she returned to the counter. "He's working on a repair. He'll be right out." She smiled at them. "Can I help you find anything while we wait on him?"

"I wish." Robin laughed. "I would take that one, I think." She pointed to an oval sapphire necklace surrounded by tiny diamonds. It was suspended on a narrow strand of silver and featured a matching set of earrings.

"You have good taste. That sapphire is a three-quarter carat in a brilliant cut. It's grade AAA and type one," the woman said. "The diamonds around it are the highest quality as well, and the setting is platinum."

Robin nodded as if she understood what that meant, though Tracy wondered if she really did. Perhaps she'd learned from a gem expert the way she had from a watch expert.

"Where would you wear something like that?" Tracy asked.

"In this hypothetical world where I can afford it?" Robin shrugged. "I'd be attending balls all the time, so I'd have plenty of opportunity to show off my jewels."

"I don't know that balls are a thing anymore," Tracy said.

"Let me dream," Robin said with a laugh.

Simon emerged from the back. He was a stooped man with big round glasses beneath thinning brown hair, and his blue and tan plaid button-down was too big for his thin frame.

A wide smile spread across his face. "Hello, Robin."

"Hi, Simon. You remember my cousin Tracy."

"Noah's daughter," he said.

"That's right." Tracy smiled at him.

"How's Velma doing?" Robin asked him.

The shop assistant vanished into the back and emerged a few moments later with a bottle of glass cleaner and a roll of paper towels.

"A little better," Simon said. "Though the days after her chemo treatments are tough."

"I'm sure," Robin said. "We're praying for her."

"Thank you," Simon said. "Now, how can I help you?"

The assistant sprayed the glass case on the other side of the store and wiped it down while they talked.

"Well, it's the strangest thing," Robin began. "You know my brother, Tom?"

"Sure. He owns the beautiful Rolex Datejust, right?"

"That's right," Robin said. "And that watch is actually why we wanted to talk to you. Tom was at Tracy's house for dinner on Sunday, and I could tell right away that his watch wasn't Grandpa Howard's Rolex. Somehow, at some point, the real thing was replaced by a fake."

Simon sucked in a breath and placed his hand over his heart. The move seemed dramatic but genuine. "What? When?"

"We don't know," Robin said. She pulled the fake Rolex from her pocket and set it on the glass.

He squinted at it then said, "Elle, could you get my loupe for me, please?"

The assistant wordlessly moved into the back of the shop once more and returned with a small round magnifying glass. She handed it to Simon and resumed cleaning.

Simon put the loupe to his eye and examined the watch, muttering under his breath. "The font is all wrong, and so is the serial number. The Cyclops lens doesn't even resemble the real thing. And the motion is so jerky. This is terrible." He lowered the magnifying glass and looked up at them. "But what happened to the real watch?"

"That's what we're trying to figure out," Robin said.

"We found the papers that show it was a real Rolex when it was purchased," Tracy said, trying to be helpful.

Simon peered at her, as if seeing her for the first time. "Of course it was real. I saw it myself. You can't mistake the real thing, papers or no."

Tracy decided not to point out that Tom had mistaken the fake for the real thing for quite some time. She supposed he meant an expert wouldn't confuse the two. From the far side of the store, she heard the squeak of paper towel on glass.

"He thinks the last time he brought it here was Christmas last year, sixteen months or so ago. He had the battery replaced, and you cleaned it for him."

"That sounds right." Simon shuffled to the register and opened a large leather-bound book. Tracy noted that it was a ledger, and on each line he had recorded a transaction in spidery blue ink. He flipped back a few pages and ran his finger down a list of names. "Here it is. Tom Peterson. Battery change and polish. And a few years before that, he needed it appraised for insurance. I did that for him. That watch was definitely the real thing when it was here."

"That's what I thought," Robin said. "Well, I guess that confirms the time frame. The real watch was swapped for a fake sometime since a year ago last Christmas."

"I hope you find out what happened to it," Simon said. "That watch was beautiful. Not to mention valuable."

"Thank you for your help," Robin told him. "At least we know more than we did before."

Robin turned to go, but the sparkly gemstones reminded Tracy of Melody's missing earrings and ring.

"Simon, do you happen to know where someone might go if they wanted to sell jewelry?" Tracy asked.

"Why? Are you interested in selling?" Simon squinted at the chip of a diamond on her left hand.

"No, not me personally," Tracy said. She tried to figure out how much to say and decided the truth couldn't hurt. "We're actually searching for some jewelry—a ring and a pair of earrings—that was stolen recently."

"Ah, you're talking about Melody Bailey's pieces? The diamond earrings and the ruby ring?"

"That's right."

"The police came and talked to me about them too. I do buy pieces sometimes—quality pieces, you understand—but I haven't seen anything like that. I sold Melody's father that ring many years ago. It was a gift to his wife for an anniversary, if I remember rightly.

To this day I would recognize that ring anywhere. It was a beauty. If anyone had brought it in here other than Melody, I would have known something was up."

"Do you know where someone might be able to sell them?" Tracy asked.

"Possibly some less-reputable jewelry stores. The thief could claim they were family heirlooms. But the only other store around here that sells anything of that caliber is the chain store at the mall, and they don't buy from customers. All their pieces come from factories." He tapped his chin. "There are always pawn shops or specialized jewelry websites."

Simon rattled off some websites that sold jewels online, and Tracy wrote them down.

"I hope you find them," Simon said.

"So do we." Robin started toward the door, and this time Tracy followed her out.

"So what did you think?" Robin asked as they walked back toward her shop.

"I believe him," Tracy said. "He seemed upset about the watch. I guess he could have been faking it, but I kind of doubt it."

"Me too," Robin agreed. "You don't make it that long in the jewelry business unless you're aboveboard."

Tracy considered what he'd said about the less-scrupulous places to unload stolen jewelry. "Do you have any desire to come to a pawn shop with me?"

"Now?"

"If you have time."

"Sure. Millie can handle the store for a while. Who's driving?"

They decided Robin would drive, and Tracy pulled up directions to the next closest pawn shop, in Quincy, on her phone. On the way there she relayed what Mitch had told her about how hard he worked to avoid selling stolen merchandise.

"If that's the case, then why does everyone keep telling us to check pawn shops for stolen merchandise?" Robin asked.

"That is an excellent question," Tracy said. "I suppose no matter how hard they try, they must end up with stolen items sometimes. And not everyone knows about the systems in place to prevent that. Anyway, let's see what we can find."

"I'm always up for an adventure," Robin said.

"Who knows? You might find some cool antiques to resell in your shop."

They fell into a comfortable silence, and as Robin drove, Tracy considered what Simon had told her. The watch had been switched out in the past year and a half. Tom had insurance on it, Simon had said. That made sense for such a valuable item, but was there any way...?

No. It wasn't possible. Tom wouldn't have pretended to lose Grandpa's watch so he could collect the insurance. He wouldn't dream of it. Besides, he and Angie both had good jobs, and no kids. They must be comfortable at least. Why would he risk committing insurance fraud?

But sometimes people were in financial trouble without giving any sign. Sometimes it appeared from the outside that things were great, but fancy labels could mean a mountain of debt, as Amy suspected of Jody. Angie had talked about how much she liked shopping, and they had mentioned they were having repairs done on the house. Had they gotten into a financial hole they were struggling to get out of? Was the watch a casualty of that? Tracy couldn't see it. But she couldn't say for sure that wasn't the situation. And Tom might not feel he could tell them the truth, that he'd sold a family heirloom, for fear of their disappointment or even anger.

A few minutes later they pulled up in front of the pawn shop in Quincy. Tracy led the way inside and to the counter. The store was larger than the one in Canton, but shabbier. The fluorescent lights sputtered, the walls appeared to be covered in a sticky yellow film, and the linoleum had white patches where the design had worn right off. The cashier sat on a stool behind bulletproof glass, watching something on his phone.

"Hello," Tracy said, trying to get his attention.

He looked up at them with a bored expression.

"We're trying to find a couple of laptops, two phones, and a ring light," Tracy said, "As well as some jewelry."

"Feel free to poke around," he said, gesturing at the shelves, where items were jumbled together with no apparent organization. Stereos sat next to golf clubs, which were next to musical instruments. Tracy didn't see her laptop, or Jeff's, or any of the other items.

"These items would have been brought in in the past few days," Robin said to the employee. "They were stolen on Saturday night. Would they be out here, or somewhere else?"

"We don't sell stolen items here." He returned to his screen.

"Is there any way we could take a peek at what's come in recently to see if our things might have ended up here by accident?" Tracy pressed.

He let out a long sigh. "I can't let you in the workroom, but I'll check for you. What did you say you were looking for?"

Tracy told him again, giving a few more details, and he exited through a door behind the counter.

While he was gone, Tracy took in her surroundings. She noted a security camera aimed at the counter and another at the door. If someone had brought in the stolen items, they would be on camera, at least.

The young man reappeared. "Nothing," he reported, settling himself on his stool once more.

"You didn't find any of them?" Tracy asked, clarifying.

"Nope." He stared down at his phone.

Tracy and Robin went back to the car. Tracy hoped the police would also be investigating the shops—and that they had more luck. The cousins found the next pawn shop easily enough, and though it offered more gold chains and sports equipment than the others, it didn't have their missing items.

"Well, at least I learned something new," Robin said. "I don't want to spend a lot of time in pawn shops."

As Robin started the car, Tracy asked, "Do you have time for one more stop?"

"I don't think I can handle another pawn shop," Robin said.

"No, nothing like that. I want to go see Sharon Presley. Pastor Gary encouraged us to visit the newcomers and make them feel welcome."

Robin smirked. "And you want to do some research."

"That too. But I truly do want her to feel welcome at the church. I wondered if you might want to come along. Didn't you say you went to school with her?"

"I did. I always liked her too. It would be fun to drop in and see her." She glanced at Tracy and then pulled away from the curb. "I think she's living with her parents for now, right?"

"She is," Tracy said. Sharon had made a joke on Saturday about being in her forties and living in her childhood bedroom. "Wait. I think she said her parents moved to a retirement community in Florida and she's renting the house from them."

"I know where it is," Robin said. "I worked with her on a group project once."

"And you still remember the location all these years later?"

"Sure." Robin shrugged. "I remember because she lived next door to a boy I liked."

Tracy laughed. "Let's swing by the bakery and pick up some cookies, and then you can take us there."

"Cookies? This errand just got better." Robin pulled onto the highway, and they drove for a few minutes in silence before she asked, "You're wondering about her son, Caleb, right?"

"Right," Tracy said. "He's come up several times as a potential suspect. I don't know if he's simply an awkward kid or what, but we know he was trying to 'get' money and he's good with technology. And he got into trouble at his old school."

"Stealing?" Robin asked.

"I don't know," Tracy said. "Sharon didn't say."

"I feel bad for the poor kid," Robin said. "I mean, we already talked about how he was the only one his age in his group, so of course he was miserable. But also, he recently lost his father and had to move away from all his friends. I'm surprised he's functioning as well as he is, frankly."

Tracy couldn't help but think that if Caleb had stolen from them, perhaps he wasn't functioning nearly as well as Robin suggested, but she didn't say so.

They soon parked at Sharon's place with the aroma of more chocolate chip cookies wafting from the back seat.

Sharon's childhood home was a midsize ranch in a neighborhood of similar homes. It had white siding and red shutters. Daffodils and hyacinth bloomed along the path to the front door. A car that was clearly several years old stood in the driveway.

Since Robin held the bakery box, Tracy knocked on the door.

Sharon opened the door moments later and beamed a greeting at them. "Hello, Tracy, Robin. It's good to see you."

"You too," Tracy said. "We wanted to say welcome to the church and let you know how glad we are you're here."

"We're the welcome wagon," Robin said, holding out the box.

"That's so sweet," Sharon said. "Come in. You'll have to forgive me. I just got home from work and changed into my comfortable clothes, since I wasn't expecting to see anyone." She gestured at her yoga pants and rumpled sweatshirt.

"You look fine." Tracy followed Sharon into a kitchen with dark wood cabinets and laminate counters. Beyond the kitchen was a dining table that held a laptop and stacks of papers. On the far side of the table were dozens of tiny brown bottles with rubber stoppers. Tracy squinted at them, trying to make out the words on the labels, but most of the space was taken up by some kind of logo with a diamond in the center.

"Do you work outside the home these days?" Robin asked.

"I work at the hair salon downtown," Sharon said. "I had my own salon back in Iowa, but this is fine until I get established here.

I'm grateful to have a job that can be done wherever we are, and I get to set my own hours, which works well with a teenager." She gestured at the bottles on the far end of the table. "I also sell essential oils on the side, hence the mess."

Tracy had met a few people who sold essential oils over the years. She knew people who made a good living from them, and also several who swore by the benefits of various oils. Approaching the bottles, she could make out the brand on the labels, which read EVERGREEN OILS.

"It sounds great." Robin set the box on the counter. "You always had the coolest hair in high school. I'm not surprised you ended up working at a beauty salon."

"I've always enjoyed helping people appear and feel their best," Sharon said, smiling. "And don't worry. I'm not going to try to sell you anything. I mean, unless you're interested, in which case I'd be happy to show you our best-selling line."

Tracy laughed. "Not today, I'm afraid."

"You must be swamped, juggling two jobs in addition to raising your son," Robin said.

"Caleb is actually pretty low maintenance. I'm so glad he's into the tech side of things. I keep telling him computer skills will always be in demand, but he doesn't want to hear it from me. All he wants to do is play video games."

"Someone has to make the video games," Robin said. "That's what I always tell my son, Kai. He's about the same age as Caleb. He doesn't think he wants to go to college, but I'm always trying to point out that if he gets a degree in game design or coding, he can play video games for a living."

"Has Caleb always been into computers?" Tracy asked.

"Pretty much," Sharon said. "Kids these days do love their screens, don't they?"

"They do," Tracy said. "I wish I knew as much about technology as they seem to."

"Me too," Sharon said.

"Is this your husband?" Robin studied a framed photo that hung on the wall over the dining table. It was of Sharon, Caleb, and a dark-haired man, posed on a beach at sunset.

"Yes, that's Leo," Sharon said. "We were on vacation in Florida last year."

"He was quite handsome," Robin said.

"He was," Sharon said. "He was so kind too."

Robin asked how Sharon had met him, and Sharon described the show choir they'd been in together in college.

Tracy let her eyes roam around the kitchen, the dining room, and the living room beyond. She didn't see any of the missing items. Then again, if Caleb had taken them, they would most likely be hidden in his room, not out in the open.

Robin and Sharon had moved on to discuss Amy's teaching job, Leo's job as a school superintendent in Iowa, and how hard it had been to move after Sharon and Leo had built a life together in another state.

Tracy tuned back in to their conversation when she heard Robin say, "Kai has been asking for an additional monitor to play his favorite game, and I'm completely at a loss for what kind he needs."

"Caleb would know," Sharon said. She gestured for them to follow her. "Let's go ask him."

Tracy understood Robin's motive. She had set up a reason for them to see inside Caleb's room.

They followed Sharon down the hallway to a door with a sign that said Keep Out. Sharon knocked and called Caleb's name. There was no answer, so she tried again. On the third try, the sound of a faint "Yeah?" came through the door. Sharon opened the door, and Tracy saw Caleb sitting in front of a computer playing some kind of video game. He had headphones over his ears and didn't take his eyes off the screen when they entered.

"What is it?" His face was scrunched up in irritation.

"Mrs. Davisson wanted to ask you for some computer advice."

Caleb's face relaxed a bit, and he slid the headphones down around his neck. "Sure. What kind of advice?"

Robin explained about Kai's favorite game, which Caleb was familiar with. Robin asked about the best monitor to get, and Caleb gave her a long and extremely thorough review of the different options. Tracy got lost quickly, so while he went on about aspect ratios and refresh rates, she looked around the room, searching for evidence that any of the missing items were present. She didn't see anything. If they were in there, they were carefully hidden.

When she turned her attention to Caleb's monologue again, he had moved from talking about monitors to talking about computers. He must have asked Robin at some point what kind of computer Kai had, because he was currently telling her that Kai really needed a different model if he wanted to be a contender in the gaming world.

After Caleb had given Robin a full rundown of the features for several computers, he recommended a specific model to her.

Tracy had never heard anyone speak as passionately or as knowledgeably about the subject before. It was abundantly clear that Caleb was obsessed with all things computers. But then, didn't most teenage boys feel the same way?

"You know, Kai has been asking for a new phone too," Robin said. "Do you know anything about cell phones?"

Caleb immediately lost his enthusiasm. His shoulders slumped, and he stared at the ground. Sharon opened and closed her mouth several times, as if struggling to come up with something to say.

"I don't really know a lot about phones," Caleb finally said, his eyes still on the floor.

"I bet you know more than I do," Robin said. "Kids your age are so much more intuitive with technology than old-timers like us. Surely you must have some ideas."

"Not really," Caleb said. "I don't know anything about phones."

"Well, Caleb, you've been really helpful," Sharon said in a too-bright voice. "We'll get out of your way now."

"Thank you for your help," Robin said.

Caleb nodded and popped the headphones back over his ears.

"Thank you for stopping by," Sharon said as they walked to the front door. "I appreciate how welcoming everyone has been. It's helped so much."

"I'm so glad," Tracy said. "Please let us know if you need anything as you settle in."

"Thank you. I will."

As soon as they were back in the car, Robin said, "That was weird, right?"

"Totally." Tracy buckled herself in. "He was fine when he was talking about monitors and computers, but as soon as you asked about phones, he clammed up."

"Sharon did too," Robin said. "That's what really stood out to me."

"I wonder what would have happened if you'd asked about diamond earrings," Tracy said.

Robin shook her head. "I don't know what happened there, but mark my words—Caleb Presley and his mother know something."

Chapter Ten

Robin parked in the small lot behind her store, and Tracy walked in through the back door with her. She figured it would be quicker to walk through the store to the street than circumvent the block of buildings.

"How was everything?" Robin called to Millie, who was straightening a pile of quilts stacked inside a steamer trunk.

"Great. We sold that 1940s radio you got in last week."

"That was quick. Who bought it?"

"Stuart Wilson," Millie replied, naming a music teacher at the middle school. "Said his wife saw it in here and told him about it. He collects radios, apparently."

"Good to know. I'll keep an eye out for radios for him," Robin said.

"I'm so sorry to hear about the theft on Saturday," Millie said to Tracy. "It's so hard to imagine someone from the church would do something like that."

"It does seem impossible," Tracy said. "Hopefully the police will figure out what happened soon."

"That's how I found out about it, actually," Millie said. "Dale Leewright and some deputy came by last night to ask if I'd seen anything. Boy, do I wish I had. I'd love to help put whoever did this behind bars. The idea of someone taking advantage of your hospitality like that makes me sick."

"Thank you, Millie," Tracy said. Millie and Arielle had been in the third group, with Robert West, Bethany Hill, Tom and Angie, and Aunt Ruth and Uncle Marvin. "You didn't notice anyone acting strangely, did you?"

Millie shook her head. "Not that I can think of."

Tracy mulled over the suspects from the third group. She figured she might as well ask, in case her questions jogged Millie's memory. "Did you get to talk much to Bethany?"

Millie appeared to think that over. "I saw her laughing a lot with Robert, but I didn't talk to her much."

"So you don't think she acted strangely at all?"

"Bethany?" Millie frowned. "I didn't see her do anything strange."

Others had, though, and Bethany had financial problems, plus that big bag. But once again, there was the fact that she had helped Tracy find a site where she might see her missing electronics. Would she do that if she was guilty? On the other hand, since the site's sellers were anonymous, Tracy couldn't rule her out. If she had sold the missing items there, she might be giving Tracy a way to get them back to ease her own conscience after selling them.

Another suspect had come up in the list of names in that third group, but Tracy didn't think it was wise to ask about Tom with Robin next to her. Robin didn't need to know Tracy harbored doubts about her brother.

"What about Arielle?" Tracy asked instead. "Did she see anything?"

"We haven't discussed it." Millie leaned back, stretching her spine.

Tracy was surprised. She didn't know Arielle very well. Arielle didn't come to visit Millie and her parents very often, so Tracy could understand why Millie wouldn't want to interrupt her sister's visit with such an unpleasant conversation, but they should talk about it. Arielle might have seen or heard something they hadn't.

"It would be nice to talk to her, to get her impressions of the night and the people there," Tracy suggested.

"Sure. I'll ask her when I see her," Millie said.

"Or if you wanted to give me her number, I could give her a call," Tracy said.

Millie pulled out her cell phone and read off a number, and Tracy entered it into her phone.

"Thanks," Tracy said. "I'll call her later." Then she faced Robin, who had already slipped behind the counter. "Thanks for coming with me today, Robin."

"Thank *you* for coming with *me*," Robin said with a laugh. "I was the one who invited you, remember?"

"I guess you're right." She chuckled and then said goodbye and walked the few blocks to the newspaper office.

"Tracy, you're back. Good," Annette said as soon as Tracy walked in the door. "Can you make a few more last-minute tweaks to the garbage story?"

The paper would go to the printer soon, so Tracy didn't have a lot of time. She quickly knocked out the changes Annette requested, helped Bethany finish the classifieds, and then she grabbed her bag and left for the night.

When she got home, Sadie greeted her at the door with a wagging tail. Tracy slipped on the leash and took her out for a walk. The trees were budding, the daffodils were in full bloom, and the air held the softness of spring. Tracy loved living in Canton all year round, but she especially loved the spring, when the world was full of promise.

Sadie sniffed at flower beds and newly-seeded lawns as Tracy walked through the streets. She passed Jody's pink house, which truly was a beauty. Was Amy right in her assertion that Jody was consumed by appearances? Was moving into one of the most visible homes in town a manifestation of that? Tracy didn't see anything wrong with living in a nice house if one could afford it, and it seemed like Jody could afford it. But what if she couldn't? What if she was in financial trouble? Amy had seen that credit card past-due notice, after all. What if she lived beyond her means and faced the consequences of that? Some nice laptops, phones, and jewelry would certainly buy her some time from the bill collectors.

Still, Tracy had seen no evidence of the theft in her home. Jody was still on the suspect list, but so were Caleb, Bethany, and—if she was honest—Tom. She and Jeff hadn't seen them at the mall when Angie had said they'd be there, and Tracy couldn't ignore that the laptop had shown up there on the Locate app, however briefly.

Come to think of it, she wasn't totally sure why Tom and Angie had joined the event in the first place. They didn't attend Faith Church and lived in another city. That Rolex might be one of the most valuable things Tom and Angie owned. If they were having financial trouble, would he have been willing to part with the watch? Had he sold it to cover their debts? Or "lost" it to collect the insurance money? The fake Rolex probably didn't cost much. Perhaps he had worn it in the hopes his family wouldn't notice the real watch was gone. But why would he do that? If he'd sold the real watch, why bring attention to it by getting a fake? He probably hadn't guessed it would be so easy for Robin to spot. Was there a chance Tom was behind the missing watch—to say nothing of the other things?

Tracy couldn't see it. Tom might be in dire enough straits to part with a family heirloom, but he wouldn't steal from others to cover his debts. And the thought of Angie as a thief was laughable. Tracy would focus on the other suspects.

She might as well call Arielle while she was at it. Tracy pulled out her phone and tapped Arielle's contact card, but the line rang through to voice mail. Tracy left a message. Maybe she would call back soon.

By the time Tracy got home, she was more confused than ever. It was a relief to set the worry about the mystery aside and focus on cooking dinner. She put together a spring risotto with asparagus, peas, and chunks of sausage. By the time Jeff got home, the dish bubbled merrily on the stove.

"The history department gave me a loaner," Jeff said, setting a laptop on the counter. It wasn't as nice or as new as his own laptop, but it was something.

"That's good of them," Tracy said. "But don't leave it there. It might get food on it."

"Okay," Jeff said, scooping it up again. "I don't know if it's good of them, exactly, or if it means they expect me to continue working on my research."

"Either way, it's nice to have."

"If the laptops don't show up in a day or two, I'll file an insurance claim," Jeff said.

After dinner and cleanup, Jeff headed to church for a meeting. As he was getting his keys, Tracy asked, "Do you think it would be okay if I used the loaner laptop?"

"I don't see why not. The password is my old one. Don't be doing any editing on the research paper I'm writing. It's open."

"The one about the Industrial Revolution?"

"That's the one."

"I'll attempt to restrain myself," Tracy said. The Industrial Revolution was a fascinating topic, but she had other plans that were much more appealing.

"I won't be late." Jeff kissed Tracy before rushing out the door.

Tracy sat down at the laptop and lifted the lid. Sadie settled at her feet as she typed in Jeff's password. The screen blinked to life, and Tracy saw that Jeff had Locate open in a tab on the screen. He'd been watching for the stolen laptops. Tracy also found their insurance company's website open in another tab.

She visited the first auction site she'd gone to, searching for any recently added laptops listed for sale in the Canton, Missouri, area. A new one had been listed by someone in Monticello, but it wasn't the right model. She also saw that the one the cat queen was selling had sold, and for a higher price than Tracy would have expected. But there was nothing like what she was anxious to find.

She changed the parameters and searched again, and then again. Before she knew it, she'd spent far too long searching for the laptops, Anna's phone, and even Tom's watch. And all she had to show for it was more confusion.

The sky was dark, and her eyes were bleary. She decided to go to bed and pray that things would be clearer in the morning.

Chapter Eleven

Tracy was pleased to see her article about the sanitation department dispute on the second page of the paper. Her column about Tully was also in its usual place. Even though it happened nearly every week—it was her job to write articles, after all—she still felt a thrill whenever she saw one of her stories in print.

"Nice work." Jeff came downstairs, straightening his tie. He gave Tracy a kiss and picked up the loaner laptop. "I read your pieces while I ate breakfast."

"Thanks. I hope the lecture goes well." She could tell by how he was dressed that it was a lecture day.

He slid the laptop into his bag. "We're talking about the causes of the Great Depression today."

She wrinkled her nose. "Sounds like a blast."

He laughed. "I hope your day goes well too." Jeff shrugged into his coat, slung his bag over his shoulder, and left.

Tracy washed the breakfast dishes, took Sadie for a quick walk, and then headed out herself. The office was quiet when she got in, as it often was the morning the paper came out. She sorted through the list of ideas people sent in for her column. There were a few interesting ones, but nothing that really jumped out at her.

She was distracted, if she was being honest. She decided to try the auction site again. It hadn't yielded anything yet, but she couldn't help herself. She needed to feel productive somehow. She opened a new tab and typed in the familiar search terms, but there was nothing new since the night before.

Perhaps she'd discover something by poking around on the site Bethany had pointed out, Resell-IT. When the site popped up, she saw that she was still logged in as Bethany. WELCOME, CIRCUITQUEEN13, it said in the corner of the screen. No matter. She wasn't planning to buy or sell anything, so it would be all right. She typed in the kind of laptop she had and ran into the same problem she'd had before. There really was no way to tell if any of the computers were hers. There wasn't anything significant or identifiable about the laptops that were for sale. She searched for Anna's phone, with the same results. Though plenty of phones were available, she couldn't tell if they were the one she was looking for. She tried the model Paula had lost. There were fewer of those, and they were lower priced, but once again, she couldn't make a positive identification.

She was about to click out of the site altogether, but when she went to close the tab, a pop-up appeared. BEFORE YOU GO, HERE ARE SOME ITEMS SIMILAR TO OTHERS YOU'VE PURCHASED. It showed pictures of several different models of computers. Bethany must have bought a laptop on the site before, which made sense, since she'd recommended it to Tracy. Before she thought too much about it, Tracy clicked on the pop-up and found herself on a page titled YOUR PREVIOUS PURCHASES, which showed about two dozen tiny photos.

Bethany had bought *all* these laptops? Tracy examined the page and realized that she hadn't merely *bought* all of them. Many of them she'd bought and resold for a profit. Tracy clicked around and found several such cases. Multiple times, Bethany had purchased a computer for fifty dollars or less then resold it afterward for up to a couple hundred dollars, making a tidy profit. But why?

"Hi, Tracy." Bethany was suddenly standing behind her. "Have you had any—oh."

Obviously, Bethany had seen that Tracy was snooping on her account. Tracy tried to justify her actions. "I was checking out that site you showed me to see if anything new came up."

"It's a great site," Bethany said, her voice unnaturally cheerful.

"I was still logged in as you, and the site prompted me to view items like ones you've bought," Tracy tried to explain.

"Well, as you can see, I use it a lot," Bethany said. "Anyway, I came over to see if you've had any luck finding the missing items."

"Not yet. Hopefully the police will uncover something today," Tracy said. Then she decided to just come right out and address the elephant in the room. "Bethany, why do you have such an interest in buying and selling laptops online?" She tried to keep from sounding accusatory, but the expression that crossed Bethany's face told her she hadn't succeeded.

"Oh, sorry, I think Eric is calling me." Bethany spun on her heel and hurried toward the boss's office.

Tracy could see through the glass walls of Eric's office. He almost never called Bethany into his office unless he was having computer problems. As the youngest member on staff, she was the de facto tech support, but since he had his back to them and was on the phone, it was unlikely that he'd called to Bethany. Her suspicion was confirmed when Bethany knocked on his office door. The young woman had made an excuse to get away from Tracy's question. She hadn't wanted to talk about why she used this website. Which, in all likelihood, meant she had something to hide.

Tracy closed her eyes and tried to think. Bethany obviously hadn't wanted to talk about what she was really doing. She was in financial trouble, if her comments about her roommate were true. And she'd had the opportunity to take all the missing items. But if she'd taken the laptops and planned to resell them on the website, why alert Tracy to its existence?

Tracy was still trying to make sense of it all when her phone rang with a call from Jeannie Morrison.

"Hi, Jeannie," Tracy said. "What's up? How's your mom doing?"

"Actually, that's why I'm calling," Jeannie said. "Last night or early this morning, a box was left at the bottom of the stairs leading to our apartment—you know, the stairs at the back of the building, not the ones inside the store. And inside it was Mom's phone."

"What?" Tracy squawked.

"Like I said, it was the strangest thing. Nothing else was with it—no note, nothing."

"Did you call Dale? Maybe there are fingerprints on it," Tracy said.

"I called him as soon as we found it, and he came and took it to the police station for examination," Jeannie said. "But I wanted to let you know too."

"I'm glad you did," Tracy said. "That's so strange."

"I know. Who would take Mom's phone and then return it?" Jeannie said. "Anna's phone hasn't been returned, has it?"

"I haven't heard that it has," Tracy said. She started to get a sinking feeling in her gut. What if it wasn't the phone itself the thief was after? What if it was the data on the phone they'd been interested in all along? The same could be true for the laptops. The machines themselves were valuable, but the information contained on them—old tax returns, banking records, lists of passwords—could be even more so. "Did your mom have a lot of apps on her phone?"

Nearly all the apps on Tracy's phone required a password to gain access. But surely that could be manipulated, if someone knew what they were doing.

"No, thankfully," Jeannie said. "She strictly uses it as a phone, so there's not a lot of her personal information on it. A small blessing."

"Or a big one."

"My theory is that Mom's phone is so old, it wasn't worth enough to bother trying to sell," Jeannie said.

"But in that case, why take it in the first place?" Tracy asked. "And why would the thief go to the trouble of returning it? Why not simply get rid of it? Even if they had an attack of conscience, why not leave it in a public place where it could be found, instead of taking it to your place and risk being seen?"

"I don't know," Jeannie said. "It doesn't make sense."

"Do you have security cameras at the shop?" Tracy asked.

"Over the door of the shop itself," Jeannie said. "We don't have any that show the back stairs to the apartment."

"That's too bad," Tracy said.

"Totally. That would solve everything," Jeannie said. "Well, I don't understand it, but I'm glad to have it back. Here's hoping the other things are found soon."

Tracy mulled over the turn of events after she ended the call. A quick call to Chad confirmed that Anna's phone had not been returned. So why had Paula's? Tracy didn't know what to think, but she didn't have much time to stew. The weekly staff meeting would begin shortly, so she gathered with the other employees in the conference room to discuss article ideas for the week. Tracy was assigned a story about a new grocery store opening in Monticello and another about a new exhibit at the Canton Historical Society.

After the meeting ended, she drove the twenty minutes to Monticello and interviewed the owner of the new store. The interview was quick and easy, and within a few minutes, she had what she would need to write her story. As Tracy left the store and got into her car, she hesitated. She could go straight back to the office and knock out the story, but on an impulse, she typed "pawn shop near me" into the search bar on her phone. There was one result, just a few blocks away.

She didn't really want to go. So far her visits to the pawn shops had left her feeling unsettled and slightly sad, and they'd yielded no leads. She wasn't sure it was worth the trouble. But how bad would she feel if she was this close and didn't check up on the pawn shop that ended up harboring the stolen items? She might as well cross another one off her list. At least then she could say she'd checked the ones she could.

She found the shop in a little strip mall between a pizza shop and an appliance repair shop. She went inside and found it was just about like the others she'd visited. The shelves were lined with abandoned golf clubs, musical instruments, jewelry, and electronics. The display of diamond rings made her the saddest of all. Every one of them was given with the promise of forever, and they had been pawned for quick cash and abandoned.

Tracy dragged her gaze away from them and spotted a girl with close-cropped hair dyed jet black behind the counter. She had several lip piercings, and her eyes were rimmed in dark eyeliner. She smiled at Tracy. "Hi," she said in a chipper voice. "How can I help you today?"

At least one part of the experience was different so far. "I'm browsing for now."

"I'm Megan. Is there anything specific I can help you find?" The girl was downright cheerful and seemed eager to help. Tracy thought about how she would be an asset to any of the more upscale stores in town.

And she would have to tell Megan what she was really after, since the items wouldn't have been there long enough to be on display in the front of the store. "I'm actually hoping to find a couple of laptops and a phone. Maybe some jewelry too. They would have been brought in sometime this week, if they're here."

Megan nodded knowingly. "I see. You're trying to locate stolen items?"

"I'm afraid so."

"We ID everyone who sells to us and work really hard to make sure they actually belong to the person who pawns them, but no system is perfect. Obviously, we don't want to be in possession of stolen items, so our policy is complete transparency in situations like this. Follow me."

Megan unlocked the door to the back of the shop and led Tracy inside. The area was smaller than the front, but it held a similar assortment of items. Tracy started by scanning the laptops for any that resembled hers or Jeff's. Then she moved on to the phones. Some older models could have passed for Paula's phone, but she didn't see anything that resembled Anna's. No ring light either.

She would never find the missing items this way, but she might as well check the jewelry case before she left. She skimmed the necklaces and rings—and the watches. She idly wondered if those Rolexes were genuine, but didn't see any that reminded her of her grandfather's watch. She did spot a ring like one she'd seen on Jody's hand the night of the dinner, which Amy told her later was expensive. A diamond tennis bracelet. A gold necklace with script that spelled out the name CHELSEA. A—

Tracy did a double take. Was she seeing what she thought she was seeing?

She pointed at the case. "Can I take a closer look at that?"

Chapter Twelve

Megan used a small key to unlock the glass jewelry case. She reached in and pulled out a ring with a teardrop-shaped ruby surrounded by tiny diamond chips. It was identical to the one in the photo Lincoln had shown Tracy on his phone. Next to it rested a pair of diamond studs.

"When was this brought in?" Tracy asked.

"Yesterday, while Jared was on duty. Do you recognize it?"

"I'm not sure, but maybe," Tracy said. "How about those earrings? When did they come in?"

"Same day," Megan said. "Jared paid for them at the same time as the ring."

This was it—the break they needed.

"I just need to make a quick call," Tracy said. She took out her phone and called Melody.

She answered right away. "Hi, Tracy. Any news?"

"I'm not sure," Tracy said. "I'm at a pawn shop in Monticello, and I found a ring that looks a lot like the one I saw in the photo of your mother. There's also a pair of diamond studs."

"Oh my. Could you send me a picture of them?"

"Hang on."

Tracy texted photos to Melody while she was still on the line.

Melody gasped. "That's it, Tracy. That's the ring."

"Are you sure?"

"Look inside the band. Is there anything engraved on it?"

Tracy flipped the ring over, exposing its gold setting. She squinted at the swirly script. "There's an *S* and a *W*."

"Serita Williams. That's my mama's ring. You found it. I can't believe you found it."

"It's probably safe to assume these are your earrings too." Tracy glanced up at Megan, who wore a pained expression. "Melody, I'll need to call you back. I'm going to hang up and call Dale Leewright."

Dale answered, and when she explained what she'd found, he promised to be there as soon as he could.

When she hung up, she found that Megan had consulted the computer and gathered not only the ring and earrings, but also a pearl necklace, a few other rings, and an opal on a gold chain. "These were all brought in together," she said, gesturing to the lot. "I'll hand them over to the police officer when he arrives. I've also pulled the ID used to sell the items."

"Who was it?" Tracy tried to tamp down the excitement in her voice.

"I'll give that information directly to the police when they arrive."

There was probably a good reason the shop wouldn't give out information like that to just anyone, but still, Tracy wanted to know who it was.

"Do you have security cameras in here?" Tracy asked.

"Yes." Megan pointed up at the cameras in each corner of the room. "I'll also give the footage to the police when they arrive."

"You couldn't give me a copy of the footage as well, could you?"

"I'm afraid not," Megan said with a tight smile.

Tracy tried to be patient, but she thought she would jump out of her skin waiting for Dale to arrive. She browsed the rest of the shelves, her eyes peeled for any sign of the other stolen items, but she didn't see anything. Still, they had found Melody's jewelry, and Dale would soon have the name and address of the thief, which meant the rest of the items would be returned shortly.

When Dale stepped inside the shop, Tracy walked over to him. "Hello."

"Hi, Tracy. Why am I not surprised that you were the one who found the missing jewelry?"

"You were the one who suggested pawn shops," Tracy said, shrugging.

"I was in here on Monday," Dale said. "And I asked the person working that day to watch out for jewelry matching this description."

"These pieces were brought in yesterday," Megan said, approaching him. "And I'm afraid the employee working Monday didn't post that information like they were supposed to. I'm sorry about that."

"We have it now," Dale said. "Thank you for cooperating."

"Thank you for coming. I have the items set aside over here." She ushered him into the room behind the counter, leaving Tracy alone in the front section of the store. They were serious about not letting her know the identity of the person who brought in the stolen goods.

Tracy waited. What was taking them so long?

At long last, Dale came back out into the front room. He carried his phone in one hand and a clear evidence bag containing the jewelry in the other. His phone screen showed a photo.

"Do you have what you need?" Tracy asked.

"Yes. And you know I can't tell you anything."

He was doing his job, but she was the one who had found the jewelry. Couldn't he give her something? Anything at all?

"Was it someone who was already under suspicion?" she asked.

"You know I can't tell you that, Tracy. You have to be patient."

Tracy knew he was right. She should stop pushing and let him do his job.

But it wasn't her fault that she could see that the photo on his phone was of a Missouri driver's license. It wasn't her fault that she could see a photo of a young woman with blond hair or that she could read the name and address. Who was Melissa Hogarth? Tracy wished she had a photographic memory, but she didn't. She did her best to memorize the address. 12001 Route C in La Grange.

"And if I find any evidence that points to the location of the laptops or phone, I'll let you know as soon as I'm able to," he added.

Phone, not phones. Which reminded Tracy—"What do you make of the fact that Paula Jordan's phone was returned?"

"I can't comment on an open investigation," Dale reminded her.

"Yeah, I know," Tracy said. After Dale left, she smiled at Megan. "Thank you for your help."

"I'm glad you were able to find your things," Megan said. "I wish they hadn't been here."

Tracy could tell that she truly cared. Megan didn't seem worried about the money the store had lost on the deal, but she was obviously dismayed that her store had been involved in such nefarious dealings.

Tracy thanked her again and went out to her car. She suspected Dale would be heading out to 12001 Route C right away, so she had a bit of time to kill so she didn't run into him.

She passed the time using her phone to research Melissa Hogarth. She typed the name into a browser window and scanned the links that came up. There were several social media profiles with similar names, but the one actual Melissa Hogarth she found lived in the UK. It was highly unlikely that she would have a driver's license with a Missouri address.

She scanned through profiles and newspaper articles but didn't find Melissa. She scrolled through images, hoping to spot a familiar face from the party on Saturday night, but with no luck. Had Melissa gotten the jewelry from one of the guests? For that matter, did Melissa actually exist? It was so rare for someone to have no digital footprint that Tracy began to wonder.

Finally, she'd exhausted all the options she could think of on her phone and decided enough time had passed that she shouldn't run into Dale.

She typed in the address and found that it was about a twenty-minute drive. She headed out, driving mostly along rural roads. She passed fields of rich earth, freshly turned and awaiting planting, as well as beautiful old farmhouses and groves of old-growth trees standing tall and proud along the creeks that fed the earth.

Finally, Tracy got onto Route C. There wasn't much here other than a few newer houses and trailers, which were set back from the road. She slowed as she got to the stretch of road where she expected to find number 12001. The narrow driveway was overgrown, but Tracy found it, and she followed it to a small trailer. The roof was partially caved in, and plants grew along the outside walls, making their way inside several of the broken windows. A piece of plywood was nailed up where the door should have been.

Whoever she was, Melissa Hogarth didn't live here. Maybe she had once, but no one had lived in this place for quite some time.

So who was Melissa, and where did she actually live? Most importantly, how had she gotten her hands on Melody's jewelry?

Chapter Thirteen

When Tracy got back to the office, she typed up her story about the new grocery store. Soon she would head to the historical society and talk to Tawny Hagstrom, the head curator, about the most recent display.

Before she did that, though, she wanted to spend a bit of time digging into the mystery of Melissa Hogarth. She started by searching the records on the Lewis County Clerk's website. After a bit of digging around, she found that no Melissa Hogarth had been born, married, bought property, or died in Lewis County in the last seventy years. She also ran a search on the house at 12001 Route C and discovered it was owned by a Steve Lappert before being repossessed by the state after he'd passed ten years ago. Was there a connection between Steve and Melissa?

She tried a genealogy website—often a gold mine of information—but didn't find any record of a Melissa Hogarth in Missouri in the last hundred years. She did find Steve, but there was no Melissa listed anywhere in his extended family tree.

It was a fake name, then. It had to be. A whole fake ID, no doubt. Tracy didn't know where one would get their hands on a fake ID, but she was pretty sure that even if she knew, the people who made them wouldn't tell her who had bought this one.

Tracy wished she'd gotten a better look at the photo on the ID, but all she could say for sure was that the picture was of a woman with blond hair.

Bethany had blond hair. Jody had enough blond highlights that she could pass for blond. Angie was blond too. But Tracy still couldn't get herself to believe that Tom and Angie would ever steal anything, which left Bethany and Jody as the only two women with blond hair on the suspect list. Was it one of them?

She needed to find another way to discover who was behind the thefts. She racked her brain, trying to make sense of it, but couldn't figure out what the best next step would be.

She packed up her purse and headed to the Canton Historical Society. She spent a pleasant hour chatting with Tawny and admiring the new display about agriculture in the area. Once she had what she needed, she said goodbye to Tawny and walked out of the old Victorian.

She knew she should probably head to the office and work on the historical society article while it was fresh in her mind. But what she really wanted to do was find out more about the new developments in the case. So far today, both the jewelry and one of the phones had been recovered, and she wanted to know how and why. She didn't know what more she could do about Melissa Hogarth, but maybe she could put some pieces together regarding Paula's phone. Tracy glanced at her watch. It was shortly past noon. She was pretty sure Paula volunteered at the library a couple of times a week. She might be there now.

Tracy had always thought it was funny that Paula volunteered at the library when her daughter owned a bookstore, but Paula had once explained that they both loved books but didn't need to work together as well as live together.

Tracy stepped into the library. A group of children was gathered for story time in the children's section, and several patrons were settled in the chairs scattered around the reading area.

Grace Park waved from behind the circulation desk. "Hello, Tracy."

"Hello." Tracy walked over to the desk and saw that Grace was loading returned books onto a cart to reshelve. "I was hoping to talk with Paula. Is she around today?"

"She is. Last I saw her, she was shelving books in nonfiction."

"I'll check there. Thanks." Tracy walked past the bank of research terminals and beyond the shelves of fiction to the nonfiction section. She looked up and down the aisles, searching for Paula. She found her poring over a heavy book about rocks and gemstones, which rested on top of a full cart of books.

"Hi, Tracy." Paula gave her a guilty grin. "I'm supposed to be putting these books away, but I keep getting distracted."

"There are worse things than getting distracted by books in a library," Tracy said.

"I suppose that's true," Paula said. "And since I'm a volunteer, they can't exactly fire me."

Tracy laughed. Paula flipped a page, and Tracy spotted a photo of several geodes, split in half to reveal crystals inside.

"I've always found rocks fascinating," Paula said. "If I'd been born a few decades later, I might have been a geologist."

Tracy was grateful that she'd been born in a time when women were allowed to have careers and pursue their passions. Women of

Paula's generation hadn't always had that freedom. Sometimes she wondered what her mother might have chosen to pursue, had she been given the opportunity.

"Jeannie called me with the good news about your phone," Tracy said. "I'm so glad it was returned."

"I am too. It's such a blessing to have it back. I don't use it all the time, but it still brings me comfort to know I can call for help if I need it."

"They are really nice to have," Tracy said. "I wondered if you could tell me anything more about how you found it?"

"Well, I went down the stairs to get the paper this morning—I always look forward to reading it on Wednesdays—and a box was sitting right outside the door. Here, let me show you." She put the gems book on the shelf in the right spot and then gestured for Tracy to follow her. "Sergeant Leewright brought it back to me a little while ago. It's in my backpack."

She led Tracy to the circulation desk and into the small staff room behind it. She took her backpack from a hook on the wall and pulled out a cell phone. "Jeannie took pictures and sent them to me." Paula held out the phone and showed Tracy photos of a small cardboard box sitting on the sidewalk right below the bottom stair. It still struck Tracy as odd. Why was the phone returned? And why was it returned that way?

Then she glimpsed something printed on the side of the box, a symbol of some kind. "May I?" Tracy asked, and when Paula handed her the phone, Tracy used two fingers to enlarge the photo.

Then she gasped. She recognized that symbol. And she knew exactly what it meant.

Chapter Fourteen

Tracy stood on the doorstep of Sharon Presley's house and rang the doorbell again. No one had answered the first time, though the car was in the driveway. Lights were on. Someone was inside. But still no one came to the door.

Tracy pulled out her phone and called Sharon. Maybe she hadn't heard the doorbell? The line rang once before going to voice mail.

Tracy didn't know what else to do, so she went back to her car and called Dale Leewright.

"Hi, Tracy." Dale sounded weary. "I can't tell you anything about the identity of the individual who brought the jewelry to the pawn shop."

"That's not why I'm calling," Tracy said. "Although, yes, I do want to know that. I'm calling about Paula Jordan's phone."

"What about it?" Dale said.

"I know it was returned last night," Tracy said. "And I know who returned it."

"You do?" Now he was interested.

"I went to see Sharon Presley earlier this week," Tracy said. "And I saw that she sells essential oils."

His tone grew dubious. "Essential oils?"

"Yes, and I saw the bottles of the oils there in her house. They have a distinctive diamond-shaped logo."

"And?"

"The box the phone was returned in has the same logo on the side." Tracy tried to keep the triumph out of her voice, but knew she hadn't quite succeeded. "The box came from Sharon's house. Which means Sharon—or, more likely, her son, Caleb, was the one who took Paula's phone."

Dale was quiet for a moment. "Hang on. I'm pulling up the photos I took of the scene. Okay, I'm looking at the box. You're saying that image is the logo for an essential oils company?"

"That's right," Tracy said. "The brand is Evergreen Oils."

"All right. And you're saying Sharon sells them?"

"Exactly," Tracy said. "I'm at her house, but she didn't answer the door, so I thought you should—"

"You went to talk to her yourself?" Dale interrupted.

"Just for a friendly visit," Tracy said.

Dale made a noise at the back of his throat. "Next time, please call me right away so I can handle it, Tracy."

"Sure thing." She knew she should feel chastised, but she was too excited. She'd been right all along. Caleb had to be behind the thefts. She'd linked him to one of them, and it was only a matter of time before she figured out how to connect him with the others.

"Are you still at Sharon's house?" Dale asked.

"Yes," Tracy said reluctantly.

"I expect you to be gone by the time I arrive to talk to Sharon."

Tracy begrudgingly agreed then hung up and drove away. She went back to the office to finish a few things, but the whole time her mind whirled, trying to make sense of the disparate scraps she'd gathered. Caleb had likely returned Paula's phone, which meant he must have taken it. A blond woman with a fake ID bearing the name Melissa Hogarth had sold Melody's jewelry to the pawn shop. Bethany had recently bought and resold a large number of used computers online. How did all the pieces connect—or did they connect at all?

Tracy kept glancing over to the front desk, where Bethany sat. Was she the woman on the fake ID? Of all the suspects, she was the most blond. But in that case, wouldn't Tracy have recognized her?

This wasn't getting her anywhere. In fact, she was starting to go around in circles. She packed up and went home. It was almost time to start dinner, and she wasn't accomplishing anything at the office anyway.

Tracy decided to make a chicken dish she'd seen online, and while she chopped vegetables and prepared the sauce to pour over the meat, she continued to puzzle over the clues she'd found.

"Hi, honey." Jeff came in, setting his briefcase on the table and hanging his coat by the door. "Do I have time to go for a quick run before dinner?"

"Sure. The chicken needs about half an hour once I put it in."

"Great."

A few minutes later, Jeff was out running and the chicken was in the oven. Tracy thought about how she should throw in a load of laundry or straighten the living room. But then her eyes fell on the briefcase Jeff had left on the table. He wouldn't mind if she used his laptop again to research a few things.

She sat down at the table and logged on to his computer. She did a search for Caleb Presley, and the usual collection of links came up—social media profiles as well as random links about various Caleb Presleys and even Elvis Presley. Nothing seemed to reference the right Caleb Presley. Tracy decided to narrow the search terms. Sharon and Caleb had moved to town from Iowa. And she was pretty sure Sharon had mentioned Des Moines at the dinner on Saturday. Tracy added the city to her search, and—

Leo H. Presley passed away on June 3 after a short battle with colon cancer, the obituary read. It listed his wife, Sharon, and son, Caleb, as survivors, as well as the funeral arrangements.

Tracy knew how hard it was to lose a parent, but she'd been an adult when her parents were killed. She couldn't imagine how it would affect a teenager to lose a parent. She was sure such a tragedy must have manifested in all kinds of ways.

She kept clicking on links and eventually somehow found her way to an online video channel hosted by someone named CryptoKing. At first she wasn't sure how it was connected with Caleb, until she saw that Caleb followed the channel and had commented on several of the videos. The CryptoKing appeared to be a man in his thirties or forties, with thinning dark hair and a mustache, and he gave advice for investing in cryptocurrency to his viewers. She didn't know too many teenagers who were interested in investing, but she supposed it wasn't so far from Caleb's other interests.

"What are you doing?"

Tracy jerked her head up. Jeff stood there, breathing heavily, his cheeks flushed from his run. "I didn't hear you come in."

"I can see that. Something obviously has you enthralled."

"I was doing research on Caleb Presley. He was the one who stole Paula Jordan's phone."

"What?" Jeff opened a cabinet door and took out a glass. "How do you know?"

Tracy explained about the logo on the box used to return the phone.

"But wait. Why are you so sure Caleb stole the phone?" Jeff asked. "And why would he return it? How do you know his mother didn't steal it?"

"My guess is that Caleb stole it and then his mother found it and returned it," Tracy said. "That would make sense, wouldn't it?"

"I don't know." Jeff filled his glass with water. "I'm merely pointing out that you don't have any real proof to say that Caleb is the thief."

Why couldn't Jeff see what was so obvious to her? "Anyway, I wanted to see what else I could find out about him."

"And what did you find? Anything that proves he was connected to the thefts?"

"I found that he's into cryptocurrency."

"Well, that's possibly a good way to lose a lot of money, but it's not illegal."

"Stealing a phone is," Tracy insisted.

Instead of answering, Jeff took a long drink of his water, emptying the glass. "What else did you learn today?" he asked after putting the glass in the dishwasher.

"How do you know I learned anything else?"

"You have that look on your face."

Jeff knew her too well. "I found Melody's jewelry at a pawn shop."

"You did?" Jeff grinned. "That's great!"

"Dale came and took the jewelry, and he'll return it to Melody. He got a copy of the ID of the person who brought it in, since the pawn shop has to keep records of that. Except I think it's a fake ID, since the name and the address on it don't check out."

"Did Dale tell you that?" Jeff cocked his head.

"Nope. I figured that part out myself. The thing we do know from the ID is that it was a blond woman who brought the items into the shop."

"But I thought you're convinced Caleb is behind the thefts?"

"He is. He must be working with the woman. Maybe the ID picture is of Sharon wearing a blond wig. She could have pawned the jewelry for him. He doesn't have any use for jewelry. He's a tech guy."

"So you're saying Caleb and Sharon worked together to steal two laptops, two phones, and jewelry—"

"And a ring light," she reminded him.

"Yes, all of that. And then Sharon, his single mother who's just come back to her hometown after her husband died, put on a blond wig and pawned the jewelry for him, but they returned one of the phones."

"The phone was too old. He couldn't use it for whatever he took the others for."

"Do you hear how unlikely this all sounds, Tracy?"

"But it's the only thing that makes sense."

"And do I need to remind you that even though you're now saying that they were in it together, just thirty seconds ago you were saying that Caleb stole Paula's phone and his mother found it and returned it?"

Tracy squirmed in her seat. "I'm just thinking out loud," she said.

"Are there any other possibilities?" Jeff asked gently. "You said the woman who brought the jewelry into the pawn shop was a blond. Who else could it have been?"

"Jody Bonilla has blond highlights," Tracy said. "And Bethany Hill is blond. So they could have had the fake ID made." No need to mention Angie.

"Okay. Do they have any relationship with Caleb?"

"Not that I know of," Tracy said.

"Let's see. Who else was there Saturday who had blond hair?" Jeff asked.

"Anna, but that doesn't make any sense. She didn't steal her own phone and ring light."

"Amy."

"Her hair is darker blond than the picture. But obviously she didn't do it," Tracy said. "She was too busy trying to wrangle all those kids to have time to steal anything."

"Sara, Grace Park, Mariella Lopez, Millie Ettlinger, and Arielle Ettlinger all have dark hair. So does Sharon, unless she put on a blond wig." He looked pointedly at her.

"Aunt Ruth, Susan, and Paula all have gray or white hair. Besides, the woman in the ID photo was not likely to be mistaken for a senior citizen."

"So it's not one of them," Jeff said. "What other women were there Saturday night? He thought for a minute and then said, "What about Angie? She has blond hair."

"Right, but she couldn't have done it, right? She's in the same category as Amy and Anna." Again, though, the doubt she had begun to feel about Tom crept in. Could it have been Angie and Tom after all? They could have worked together to steal the items, and Angie could have pawned the jewelry. She could be the woman in that photo ID.

"I don't know," Jeff said with a shrug. "I'd like to think not. But don't you need to consider every possibility?"

Tracy didn't want to consider that one. But she couldn't ignore the doubts that had started to swirl in her mind. First there was the thing about the shopping center then the questions about the missing Rolex. Was there any chance her cousin and his wife were up to no good?

She decided she needed to find out more about what was going on with Tom and Angie.

Chapter Fifteen

Thursday morning was misty, with a blanket of clouds hanging low in the sky. Tracy woke up with a list of tasks on her mind that she wanted to complete. After breakfast, she called Angie and invited her and Tom over for dinner that evening. Angie agreed with delight, so Tracy ran out to the grocery store as soon as she hung up. She'd been planning tacos for herself and Jeff, but now that Angie and Tom were coming over, she wanted to make something a little nicer. She bought ingredients for a spring pea tart made with herbs and ricotta that she'd been wanting to try.

Once she got home and put away the groceries, she realized Arielle Ettlinger hadn't returned her call, so she tried calling again. Tracy didn't honestly think she'd had anything to do with the thefts—she hadn't done anything suspicious, she had no real motive, and she had dark hair—but it bothered her that Arielle was one of the few she hadn't yet spoken to about the events of Saturday night. The call went to voice mail, and Tracy left a message, again asking Arielle to give her a call.

Speaking of people she hadn't talked to… Tracy drove to PJ's, a staple in town, and walked into the breakfast café. Over the decades, patrons had carved their initials and declarations of love into nearly every square inch of the dark wood paneling, and over time the carvings had become part of the restaurant's charm.

Tracy went to the counter and found Robert West sitting on his familiar stool, drinking coffee. Robert spent most mornings on that stool, reading the paper and chatting with anyone who came by.

Tracy took the seat next to him. "How are you today, Robert?"

"Hello, Tracy. The Lord woke me up this morning, so I'm doing all right. How about you?"

"I'm fine." She smiled up at the waitress, who offered her a menu. "Just coffee for me, please."

The waitress took the menu away and a moment later slid a cup of coffee in front of her along with a little dish of creamer pods and another of sugar packets.

Tracy thanked her and doctored her coffee then returned her attention to Robert. "I wanted to talk to you about Saturday night."

"I wondered when you would get around to me." Robert grinned over the rim of his coffee cup. "It sounds like you've talked to pretty much everyone else in town about it. What, you don't think I seem like a viable suspect?"

Tracy laughed. She stirred her coffee and took a sip then asked, "Do you know what a hard drive is?"

"No, but for the right price, I could figure it out," Robert said, smiling. "That doesn't mean I might not want a shiny new laptop. I could carry it around so I look young and cool, like the kids do."

"That would be very convincing," Tracy said, trying to keep a straight face.

"I do have a cell phone," Robert said. "My grandson Linton got it for me. He said it would make me safer. The problem is that I can never remember to turn it on, so it doesn't do me much good."

"I've got to be honest, you don't sound like the most likely thief," Tracy said. "Since most of the items taken were electronics, we're thinking the culprit is probably tech-savvy."

"Fine." Robert feigned disappointment. "But I'm afraid I can't help you figure out who it is. I didn't see anything suspicious that night."

"Nothing?" Robert had been in the third group, with Millie and Arielle, Aunt Ruth and Uncle Marvin, Tom and Angie, and Bethany. Kevin had reported that Bethany had vanished for a long stretch, and Bethany had admitted to having a text fight with her roommate. "You didn't notice anyone acting strangely, or disappearing for a long time, or—"

"Stuffing a laptop under their coat?" Robert suggested it with a straight face, but his eyes twinkled with mirth.

"Right. You didn't see anything like that?" Tracy asked.

"I did not." Robert drained his coffee. No sooner had he set down the empty cup than the waitress appeared and refilled it.

"I noticed you chatting with Bethany Hill," Tracy said. "Did you know her before?"

"Not at all," Robert said. "But we started talking at the first stop, and we got along like a house on fire. She said I reminded her of her grandfather."

"I'm so glad." Tracy loved seeing people unexpectedly become friends. "Did you two talk about anything interesting?"

"Well, she listened to me go on about my grandkids, so that was nice. She also asked about being a ferryboat captain, and I enjoyed telling her about all that. And she told me about her roommate problems and how hard it is to make it in journalism and about her art."

"Her art?"

"Sure. Have you seen it? It's really neat."

"I didn't know Bethany is an artist."

"She showed me some of her stuff on her phone. It's all very high-tech, of course—not like what we would have called art in my day—but Rachelle says I need to change with the times. And it's definitely cool."

"What's it like?" Tracy drank more of her coffee.

"It's got computer parts in it. Lots of shiny bits on a canvas, mixed up with paint and who knows what else. She says it's a commentary on the madness of the modern world. I don't know about all of that, but it is interesting. You could find it on her website if you wanted to."

"Do you know what her website is?" Tracy had researched Bethany, but an art website hadn't come up.

"Circuit Queen, or something like that. I'm sure she'd be happy to tell you. She seemed keen to sell some of it. I get the sense she could really use some income on the side. They must not be paying her enough at the paper."

Tracy pulled out her phone and did a search for *CircuitQueen.com*. It was very close to Bethany's username for Resell-IT. A sleek website came up, with a white background punctuated by pictures of canvases that had circuit boards and computer chips worked in alongside the paint. "Wow."

"That's it," Robert said, peering over her shoulder at the screen. "That's her website."

It was strange, and kind of messy. But it was also unexpectedly beautiful, the way the intricate wiring and rainbow sheen of the electronics parts mixed in with the paint. "It's really nice."

"I'm not saying I would want to hang it on my wall, but it's certainly unique. Not the same old word art or smiling cherubs everyone has."

"It is indeed." It also meant that there was an explanation for Bethany's buying old computers online. She took them apart and used them for her art. That didn't necessarily mean she couldn't also have stolen the laptops and phones to use to make a piece—the allure of free parts must have been tempting—but it did mean that some of the behavior that had struck Tracy as strange really did have a logical explanation. And if Robert was right, she was trying to sell her art to help alleviate her financial problems, which lined up with what Bethany had told her about her roommate.

"I don't think Bethany stole those laptops to make her art, if that's what you're thinking," Robert said, as if reading her mind. "I know it does kind of make her look guilty, now that I've shown you that she has a purpose for computer parts, but I don't see her doing that."

"I agree with you," Tracy said. It wasn't impossible, but it certainly didn't make a lot of sense. It didn't feel like the right solution, even if Bethany was one of the few who could be the woman on the fake ID. Tracy wouldn't take her off the suspect list entirely, but she would focus her energy on other possibilities.

"I do hope you find the thief, whoever it is," Robert said. "It's a terrible thing when people can't welcome members of their church into their homes."

"Thank you." Tracy gestured to the waitress, who slipped her the check. Tracy paid for her coffee and Robert's. "I hope so too. You'll let me know if you think of anything that might be important, won't you?"

"You know I will." Robert's eyes crinkled at the corners as he smiled.

"Enjoy your day." Tracy headed outside, pulling her coat closer as she walked to her car.

She drove to the bakery and loaded up on breakfast pastries and coffee then drove to the police station. The next item on her list was to try to get an update from Dale. If he'd learned anything about the person behind the fake ID, maybe it would lead back to her laptop.

Inside a quiet police station, she found the police sergeant at his desk, munching on a bagel and drinking coffee from a paper cup. He gave her a wry smile and set down his bagel. "Hi, Tracy. What's up?"

"I come bearing gifts." She held out the pastries and fresh coffee.

"You must be hoping for an update." Dale eyed her, waiting.

"I can't bring a friend some treats to thank him for a job well done?" she asked innocently.

He chuckled and accepted the bakery goods. "There's not really much I can tell you, Tracy."

Tracy perched on the chair he kept for visitors. "I know that Melissa Hogarth isn't real. It's a fake ID, isn't it?"

Dale stared at her. "How did you know the name on the ID?"

"I have excellent detective skills." Tracy didn't need to tell him how he'd accidentally let that information slip. "But I haven't been able to figure out who at the dinner used the fake ID."

"Even if I knew that, I couldn't tell you." He selected a pastry. "No matter how many cream horns you bring me."

"But you must have some leads."

"Tracy, please trust us to do our jobs."

"I do trust you," Tracy said. "And I appreciate all you're doing. But I was the one who found the jewelry. Can't you tell me anything about the person who pawned it?"

Dale was silent for a long time, clearly debating as he polished off the cream horn. At last he said, "What I can tell you is that the name on that ID is not new to us. Several credit cards have been opened under the name Melissa Hogarth, and large debts run up. Whoever is behind that name has been on law enforcement's radar for a few months."

"Really?" She couldn't imagine any of the party guests doing something like that—until she thought about Jody and her piles of boxes with high-end labels. Could she have bought some of those luxury items with stolen credit cards? It didn't really sound all that far-fetched. And Jody had only lived in town for a few months, so the time frame also pointed to her. Plus, she was one of the suspects with blond hair.

"We've already been working with the merchants where the cards were used around here," Dale said. "To try and get security images or any other information that would help make a positive identification."

"What about the security camera at the pawn shop?" Tracy asked. "Did that help at all?"

Dale sighed. "A woman wearing a hat and sunglasses came into the shop and pawned the jewelry. The employee who was working at the shop at the time wasn't quite as sharp as the woman who helped us. He wasn't as careful as he should have been."

"He didn't make her take off the hat and sunglasses?"

"He did ask her to lower her sunglasses for a moment, but there's not enough for us to get any real information from the video. We've spoken to him, but he couldn't tell us much about her."

"He doesn't sound like a very attentive employee."

"I don't think he'll be working at that shop much longer," Dale said. "In any case, the footage wasn't as helpful as we would have liked. But we're investigating, Tracy, and as I've told you before, I'll let you know when I have something to report."

Tracy had to take Dale at his word. There was nothing else she could do. She thanked him and went out into the sunshine.

She had one last stop to make before she headed to the office, and it was the one she was most nervous about. Still, it had to be done, so she hurried to Great Lengths Salon and was glad to see through the large front window that Sharon was there.

Tracy pulled the door open and went inside. The tang of chemicals and the scent of bleach was partially masked by a floral fragrance from the diffusers set around the room. Big globe lights hung from the ceiling, and the bold floral wallpaper along one wall was set off by a wall of plants in tiny macrame containers on the other side of the salon. A young woman with curly red hair stood behind the counter, and Sharon straightened bottles and jars in front of one of the chairs.

When Sharon looked up and saw her, Tracy saw fear in her eyes. She froze for half a second before she recovered herself and plastered on a smile. "Hi, Tracy."

"Hi. I was hoping I could talk to you," Tracy said.

"I'm expecting a customer soon," Sharon said, gesturing at the chair.

"This won't take long," Tracy said. "I just want to ask you about something."

Sharon opened her mouth as if to argue, but then it seemed the fight went out of her. "Let's go in the back."

Tracy followed her into a small break room in the rear of the salon. A table and chairs were set up there, along with a microwave and minifridge.

"I wanted to ask you about Paula Jordan's phone," Tracy said.

Sharon bit her lip then said, "We were hoping no one would figure out who left it there."

"What gave it away was the logo on the side of the box," Tracy said. "I recognized it from the essential oils line I saw at your house."

Sharon slapped a hand to her forehead. "I didn't think of that."

"It was a good thing you returned the phone," Tracy ventured, hoping it would coax Sharon to explain.

"Caleb didn't steal it," Sharon said. "And neither did I. He found it in his backpack. We were hoping to return it quietly so no one would think more was going on than there really was."

"What do you mean, he found it in his backpack?" Tracy asked.

"He was digging through it the other night for a pencil, and the phone was there. Neither of us knew whose it was or how it got there. It didn't belong to anyone I knew, and no one Caleb's age has a phone that old. The battery was dead, but it took the same charger my phone takes, so we plugged it in and turned it on to see the contacts or anything else that would help identify it. Paula didn't have any kind of screen lock set up, so it didn't take us long to find out it was hers."

"How did Paula's phone end up in Caleb's backpack, if he didn't take it?" Was Sharon one of those parents who couldn't see their child's bad behavior until it was too late?

Sharon shrugged. "Paula had a black backpack that was very similar to Caleb's on Saturday night."

Tracy thought about it for a moment and realized she was right. Paula carried a backpack because purses were too hard on her shoulder.

"We think she must have put her phone in Caleb's bag by accident."

The theory made sense. Paula was anything but doddering or feeble, but if there was a jumble of bags by Pastor Gary and Kathy's door, as there had been at Tracy's house, she could see how someone would mistake one black backpack for another.

"But why didn't you just tell Paula what had happened?" Tracy asked.

"Because once we found it, we knew what everyone would think." Sharon crossed her arms over her chest. "I'm not stupid. I know why you were at our house asking about monitors and computers and phones. When Caleb found the phone, we knew everyone would think he stole it and everything else."

Tracy had to admit Sharon was right. After all, it was exactly what she had thought.

"Caleb isn't the most social kid, and his people skills aren't great. He probably spends too much time playing video games, and he's certainly made mistakes. But he's not a thief, and he didn't steal Paula's phone or anything else."

She said it with such conviction that Tracy was inclined to believe her. And Sharon's logic was solid. Tracy *had* thought Caleb was guilty when she figured out who had retuned the phone. Would she have suspected him less if they had simply returned the phone to Paula with an explanation about what had happened? Maybe. But she couldn't say for sure that she would have. She hated to admit it, but she could see why Sharon had thought returning the phone in secret was the best strategy.

"So you don't know anything about the other stolen items?" Tracy asked feebly.

"I don't, and neither does Caleb," Sharon said firmly. "I would love to know who did take them. It burns me up to think that someone took advantage of your hospitality like that. But if you think it was me or my son, you're barking up the wrong tree."

This time Tracy truly believed her. Which meant yet another suspect crossed off her list.

But if it wasn't Caleb, then who was it?

Chapter Sixteen

Tracy tried calling Arielle as she walked back to her car, but it rang through to voice mail again. She left another message, but she still hadn't been able to talk to the young woman, and she was starting to wonder why. She hadn't considered Arielle a suspect, but it was starting to seem strange that she wouldn't return calls. Tracy didn't know if Millie would be working today, but Pearls of Wisdom was on her way to the office anyway.

She stepped inside the shop and found Robin behind the counter, talking on the phone. Robin waved, and Tracy waved back. She spotted Millie dusting a display of glassware and made her way toward her.

"Hey, Millie," Tracy said.

"Hi, Tracy." Millie faced her but waited a bit too long before she smiled. "How are you?"

"I'm all right," Tracy said. "But I haven't been able to get ahold of Arielle. I was wondering if you know what's going on or if there's another way I might be able to get in touch with her."

"That's odd," Millie said. "Have you been calling her, or texting her?"

"Calling," Tracy said.

Millie pressed her lips together. "Try texting her. She hates talking on the phone. When I text her she usually texts right back."

"Okay," Tracy said. She would try that, but she needed more help from Millie. "Could you let her know I'm hoping to talk with her and ask her to call or text me? She's still staying with you and your parents, right?"

"I'll tell her," Millie said. "I'll let her know when I see her."

"Great. Thanks."

Tracy waved again at the counter and started toward the door, but Robin called out, "Hang on!"

Robin set the phone back in its cradle and came around the counter toward Tracy. "That was a dealer in Hannibal I've worked with a bunch of times. I called him to ask whether he'd seen a watch like Tom's in recent years and if he could ask the people he knows who specialize in watches if they've seen one like it."

"That's a great idea," Tracy said, though secretly she figured it was probably a needle in a haystack. Antique watch dealers must see hundreds if not thousands of watches in a year. How would they possibly remember seeing a specific one, even if it had found its way into legitimate sales channels? "What did he say?"

"He said he doesn't remember seeing any Rolex Datejusts from the fifties, but he'll go through his records and ask his colleagues if they've seen anything. He'll get back to me as soon as he can."

"That's great. Let's hope he finds something," Tracy said.

"I'll let you know what he says," Robin promised.

Tracy said goodbye, drove to the newspaper office, and made her way to her desk. The office was quiet. Eric was on the phone, both Bethany and Jake were out somewhere, and Annette was busy on her computer.

Tracy sat down and sorted through her emails. Annette had asked her to work on a story about higher water bills. That shouldn't be hard to bang out. And then she could start on the piece about the historical society. After that, she would research the history of the building that housed Ballard's Drugstore. There were rumors of Underground Railroad tunnels beneath it and a small possibility that it could have been one of the stops on the famed Mary Meachum Freedom Crossing. Though Tracy had never heard of any evidence that pointed to that possibility, she was eager to find out once and for all for her column.

Before she got started on that, she did her now-regular searches on the auction site, checking on new laptops listed for sale in the area. She wasn't surprised to find that none of the new laptops matched hers or Jeff's. She also used Locate to see if she could determine where her missing laptop was, but no dice.

She would focus on getting the articles done, and then she would cut out a bit early to get started on cooking dinner for Tom and Angie. At least the day didn't have to be a total bust.

She tried to ignore how the idea of suspecting her cousin turned her stomach so much that she didn't see how she'd eat a single bite that evening.

Chapter Seventeen

In spite of her traitorous mind's insistence on focusing anywhere but where it should, Tracy managed to finish a draft of both articles. She got home early enough to get the tart in the oven and clean the kitchen. Jeff set the kitchen table, which felt much more comfortable for a small casual meal than the big dining room, and a tray of cheese and crackers waited on the counter alongside teal cocktail napkins.

The doorbell rang, and when Jeff went to let their guests in, Tracy took a deep breath to brace and calm herself. This was her cousin and his wife, and she loved them no matter what. But she was having doubts, and she needed to find out what was going on with them. It was crazy to even suggest they might have had anything to do with the thefts, but she was running out of alternative explanations. Even if they weren't behind the thefts, perhaps something was happening for which they could use familial support. Either way, she would see what she could learn tonight.

"Hi, Tracy." Angie carried a bouquet of flowers wrapped in paper from a local florist, and she handed them to Tracy. Angie smiled, but she appeared tired and unfocused. Something wasn't right with her. "Thanks so much for inviting us over. We haven't spent nearly enough time together on this visit."

"Thank you for coming." Tracy hugged Angie. A moment later, Tom appeared behind her, and Tracy also gave him a hug. "It's so good to see you both. Help yourselves to some cheese and crackers while I put these in water." She gestured at the tray. "Dinner's almost ready."

"It's good to see you. We love this about Canton," Angie said. "Being able to drop over to see family on a weeknight. We can't do that kind of thing in Lincoln, and we miss it."

"You can always move back," Jeff said, coming into the kitchen behind them. "Then you could be here all the time."

There was a heavy pause, and then Angie laughed. "I wish. That sure would be nice."

"If only," Tom added, but his tone was awkward. "It's hard to believe how quickly our visit has gone."

Tracy glanced at Jeff. Was there something odd, stilted, about how they'd responded? But if there was, Jeff didn't seem to notice, as he was busy pouring water from a pitcher into glasses for them.

"Would you ever consider it?" Tracy asked. "Moving home, I mean." She took down a vase and added water.

"Sure," Tom said. "If circumstances aligned, we'd love to. But we'll have to see about that."

"Tracy, I really enjoyed your article in the paper this week," Angie said. Was she trying to change the subject?

"The one about garbage collection?" Tracy joked.

Angie nodded. "I mean, garbage collection isn't anyone's favorite subject, but I loved reading about such a small-town kind of thing."

"Oh. Thank you." Tracy didn't totally understand the comment. Garbage collection was something all cities dealt with. It wasn't unique to small towns.

Maybe she was being too suspicious, when Angie was just trying to give her a compliment. Tracy peeled off the florist paper and plastic around the flowers. The arrangement included deep purple dahlias, bright pink peonies, white lilies, and some beautiful greenery. She loved it.

"What have you been up to while you've been here?" Tracy asked, hoping to steer the conversation toward some answers.

"Mostly seeing family," Angie said. "We've been able to spend some time with Ruth and Marvin as well as Robin and Terry and my parents."

"Have you been able to get in any more shopping?" Tracy used scissors to trim the stems, sliding each one into the vase after.

Angie's eyebrows rose. "Shopping?"

Why was she confused about that? Tracy's inner antennae perked up. "On Sunday after church, you said you were going to the shopping center," she said, keeping her tone neutral. "You said you love shopping."

Angie laughed, but it sounded strained. "I do. And we did. We had a great time shopping there on Sunday."

"Sounds like a successful trip," Tracy said. "What stores did you go to?"

"The hardware store," Angie said.

"The bookstore," Tom said at the same time.

"We went to both," Angie added quickly. "All our favorite places."

Something was definitely off about their story. What was going on? There wasn't even a bookstore in that shopping center, so Tom was lying. But why?

"Have you been to any of the newer stores downtown?" Jeff asked, holding out a glass of water for Tom. "I especially like Jeannie

Morrison's bookstore, Huckleberry Books. She's always really good about helping me with hard-to-find history books."

"And I love the secondhand shops in particular," Tracy said. "They're great places to buy and sell used items. Much easier on the wallet."

Angie and Tom were smiling, but Jeff stared at her as if she'd lost her mind.

Tracy ignored him and continued. "Like Pop Rocks Vintage. Whitney has some really cute clothing. She buys a lot of the things that people find in their attics. Have you ever sold something to a secondhand shop?" Angie's brow furrowed, so Tracy said, "You know, like jewelry or maybe clothing from when we were teens."

"I haven't," Angie said. "But that's a good idea. I should go through my things and find a place in Lincoln that might buy them."

"Pawn shops too," Tracy said. "I've discovered the local pawn shops recently, and you can find so many good-quality things at steep discounts there."

"I've never been inside a pawn shop," Angie said.

"I hadn't either until recently," Tracy said, trying to read Angie. Was she telling the truth? "You can pawn your items to get quick cash, but if you don't return to buy them back, they go up for sale, and anyone can buy them."

Tom looked at her like she had two heads. "I guess next time I'm looking for something, I can check a pawn shop first."

Jeff came to her rescue. "Fortunately, it's such a beautiful time of year to be here, no matter what you're doing." He held out a glass for Angie.

"It really is," Tom said, relief washing over his features.

"It's so nice that you were able to get away from work," Tracy said.

"I'm lucky that my job is flexible," Tom said. "I can do accounting from anywhere, so I've been working a few hours a day while we've been here."

"My job isn't flexible at all, at least not the location," Angie said. "I have to be at the hospital for it." She was an emergency room doctor, so Tracy could see her point. "But I had a lot of vacation days saved up, so I've been able to get away completely, which has been nice. With such a high-stress job, sometimes you have to leave the state to remember there's a world outside of work."

"How is work going?" Tracy asked as she finished transferring the bouquet into the vase.

"Busy," Angie and Tom both said at once. They looked at each other and laughed.

"But good," Angie added.

"For me as well," Tom said. "How is it at the college, Jeff? I heard budget cuts are hitting higher education pretty hard these days."

Angie excused herself to use the bathroom before they sat down, and Jeff discussed his colleagues in the history department as Tracy got dinner on the table. Angie returned, and they all took their seats. As they ate, Angie asked about the newspaper, so Tracy talked a little about the changes that had happened when the new editor-in-chief had taken over. Angie merely picked at her food, nibbling the pastry crust without really touching the rest of it. Didn't she like vegetables? Tracy had thought she did.

She decided it was time to broach the next topic that burned in her mind. "Have you had any luck finding out what happened to Grandpa's watch?"

"No." Tom cut off a bite of the tart. "I did talk to Larry, the contractor who's been working at our house, and he insisted he hasn't seen it since the day I showed it to him."

"And you believe him?" Tracy asked.

Tom shrugged. "He has the keys to our house. I wouldn't have given him those if I didn't think he was honest."

"It's so frustrating to not know what happened to it," Angie said. "Where could it have gone? Who could have taken it?"

"The fact that it's valuable doesn't even matter," Tom added. "I would never have sold it, so the cost is immaterial. The sentimental value far outweighs any money we could have made from it."

"It's terrible to think your grandfather's watch is lost," said Angie. "That piece of family history is gone, and now it can't be passed down to the next generation."

They could be lying. It could all be an act. But Tracy didn't think it was. From the way Angie spoke, the loss obviously pained her. It wasn't even her family's heirloom, but it clearly mattered to her as if it were.

"I saw Robin briefly today, and she told me she's talking to a dealer in Hannibal she works with," Tracy said. "He's going to check his records and ask around to see if anyone he knows has seen the watch."

"Let's hope that turns up something," Angie said. "But I don't see how it could if he's local. It's likely that the watch went missing in Lincoln, and I have no idea where to start searching for it there if that's the case."

"I still can't believe I didn't notice," Tom said. "Now that Robin has pointed it out, it's so clear that this is a fake. I can't imagine how I ever thought it was real."

"Robin is an expert," Tracy said. "She's trained to notice things like that."

"And it is a pretty good fake, honestly," Angie said.

"I just can't believe it's gone," Tom said. "I'm still wearing this one because I'm used to having something on my wrist to check the time, but it feels awful. Every time I look at it, I'm reminded how I failed Grandpa and Uncle Noah."

"You didn't fail anyone," Tracy told him firmly. "It's entirely the fault of whoever switched out the watches. They bear sole responsibility for this."

Tom gave her a small smile. "Thanks, Tracy."

The conversation moved on, and by the time Tracy brought out the pound cake she'd made for dessert, she was confident that Tom hadn't sold the watch. But she still wasn't sure what they'd been doing at the shopping center that day—if they'd even been there, as they'd claimed. There was something fishy about all of it. She didn't know whether they'd had anything to do with the missing laptops and watches, but she did know that something strange was going on. There was something they weren't telling her.

And Tracy was determined to find out what it was.

Chapter Eighteen

Tracy had just parked at home after work Friday afternoon when she got a call from Robin.

"Hey, Robin," Tracy said. "What's up?"

"I heard back from my friend, the antique jewelry dealer."

"What did he say?" Tracy stepped out of the car and shut the door behind her. Sadie's face appeared in the window, and Tracy waved to her.

"He invited me to come by his shop in Hannibal tomorrow."

"For what? What did he find out?"

"I don't know, but I assume he'll tell us tomorrow. I invited Tom, but he and Angie have plans."

"They have plans on a Saturday morning that are more important than finding the watch?"

"Apparently," Robin said. "He didn't say what, even when I pressed, so I don't know what's going on with them. I even asked Mom, and she said she had no idea what they were up to. But whatever. Since he can't come, I wondered if you wanted to."

Hannibal was a river town about forty minutes south of Canton, famous as the boyhood home of Mark Twain.

"Of course I do. When?" She slung her bag over her shoulder, closed the car door, and walked toward the house.

"His shop opens at ten, and he says earlier in the day is better, so we'd have to leave early."

"I'll be ready."

"Great. I'll pick you up a little after nine."

"See you then." Tracy ended the call.

Sadie greeted Tracy with her usual effusive joy, and Tracy set her bag down and clipped the leash to the dog's collar. "You ready to go for a walk?"

Sadie darted to the door in response. Outside, the air was warm and sweet. The curious goldendoodle sniffed at the flowers and the grass, and Tracy ran into her neighbor Lisa, also out for a walk on a warm spring afternoon. They chatted for a few minutes, and then Tracy headed home.

She unclipped Sadie's leash and fed her. Tracy had agreed to babysit for Kevin and Sara that night so they could go out for their anniversary, but she had some time before she had to leave. She checked the online auction site to see if any new laptops were listed. There were two, one listed by someone named FancyCat and another by a seller who went by OrangeJerry. But neither of them matched Tracy's or Jeff's laptops.

She thought about calling Dale to see if there was any update on the person behind the fake ID who had sold the jewelry to the pawn shop. He'd promised to keep her updated, but it wouldn't hurt to ask in case he'd found something and forgotten to call her.

"Hi, Dale," Tracy said when he picked up.

"Hey, Tracy. I don't have any update on the laptops, I'm afraid."

"I was actually calling to see if you had any news about the person behind Melissa Hogarth," Tracy said.

"You know I couldn't tell you even if I did," Dale reminded her. "What I can tell you is that we're still reviewing security footage from the stores where Melissa Hogarth's fraudulent credit cards were used. We're hoping to have answers soon." His phone cut out for a second. "I have to go, Tracy. I'm getting a call on another line."

"Okay." Tracy hung up, resigned. She got started on dinner and had the salad almost done when her phone rang with a call from Jeff.

"Hi," she said. "What's up?"

"Your computer is online. I was on Locate for one of my regular checks, and it's there. It's online."

"Oh my goodness. Where is it?"

"In Massachusetts."

Tracy's mind spun. "What is it doing there?"

"Your guess is as good as mine. I took a screenshot, and I've already contacted Dale—"

"It was you!" Tracy interrupted.

"What?"

"When I was on the phone with Dale a few minutes ago, he said he had to go because someone was calling him. It was you."

Jeff chuckled. "I guess it was. Anyway, I let him know the laptop is in Massachusetts. You know how the app gives an address for the location of the item?"

"Yeah." The app wasn't always completely accurate, but most of the time it was able to give at least a ball park idea of where an item was.

"Apparently, your laptop is in a place called Sandwich, Massachusetts, in an area where the houses are rather far apart. So it's likely it has the right place. Dale is going to try to track down a phone number, which will be easy enough if there's a landline. Then he'll let us know what he finds out."

Tracy grinned. "That's wonderful news, Jeff!"

"I hope this is really it," Jeff said. "It would be great to get your laptop back."

"It really would. Let's hope Dale finds it." She paused for a moment. Dale was on it, but she couldn't stop herself from asking, "What's the address?"

Jeff rattled off the address. "And I can tell you're going to do some sleuthing of your own. Please do not buy a plane ticket to Massachusetts."

"I won't." But she would if she could.

"Okay then. Let me know what you find out."

"I will." Tracy hung up and tapped her screen to research the address Jeff had given her. Her phone was much less useful for this kind of thing than her computer. She couldn't wait to get it back. Still, she easily located a real estate listing that depicted a gray house with dormer windows, a big yard, and a tennis court. It was surrounded by mature trees and butted up against a forested area. The house appeared to be on a gravel road, though it was clearly well maintained. Tracy clicked around on the street view and found that at the end of the road was a beautiful beach. That alone would raise the value of the nearby homes, including the one she was interested in.

If the house had a landline, it shouldn't be hard to find the owner's number. She pulled up another search window and searched the address again, along with *phone number*. She found an online listing for the address. It couldn't hurt to call, could it? She'd just see what they said. She dialed the number before she could talk herself out of it.

"Hello? Ruben Carter here. Is this the police again?" The man sounded older, and he had a thick Boston accent.

"No, it's not the police," Tracy said. "My name is Tracy Doyle, and I'm calling from Canton, Missouri."

"That's where the police officer was from," he said. "You have the same area code, so I figured."

"I'm not with the police," Tracy said. "Did the police officer from Canton call you about a laptop?"

"That's right," Ruben said. "About the one I bought. He told me it was stolen."

"I'm afraid it was," Tracy said. "It belongs to me."

"I'm sorry to hear that," he said. "I had no idea. I would never have bought it if I had known. The listing said it was used, but it didn't occur to me that it could have been stolen."

"Of course it didn't," she assured him. "How could you have known that?"

"I'll return it, naturally," he said. "And I've filed a complaint with the website. I'll expect a full refund from them."

"They should have to give you at least that," Tracy said. "They should make sure they're not selling stolen goods."

The man sighed. "My daughter is always talking about how great it is to buy things online, but I don't know. This has certainly soured me on the whole thing."

"Not all online shopping experiences are bad, but I'm sorry that this one didn't work out well," Tracy said. "Did you buy it on an auction site?"

"I did," he said. "It was smooth enough at first. It was a very good deal. That probably should have been my first sign something was wrong. The price was way below the others listed for sale. But it was easy. I clicked to buy it, and the seller sent shipping info right away. It came quickly and was in great shape when it arrived. Everything seemed legit. But obviously that wasn't really the case."

"Would you be able to send me the interactions you had with the seller?" Tracy asked. "The listing, shipping info, and anything else they sent?"

"Sure," he said. "I'm already sending it to the police. I can send it to you as well."

"Thank you so much." She gave him her email address and phone number, and he apologized again.

"It's not your fault," Tracy said. "Thank you for being honest about the whole thing. Not everyone would have been willing to work with the police in this situation."

"I don't want to encourage or reward theft," he said firmly. "I'll do whatever I can to help you all find whoever did this. I'll send this information along after I take my dog for a walk."

Tracy thanked him again and hung up. She couldn't do anything more about the situation until Ruben sent the information about the seller, so she decided she might as well get ready to head over to Sara and Kevin's. She left instructions for reheating last night's tart for Jeff then climbed into the car.

Sara and Kevin lived in an old farmhouse a few miles outside of town. Kevin's parents, David and Susan, lived at the neighboring farm and watched the kids most days while Sara and Kevin worked. Sometimes Tracy was envious of how much time they got to spend with the grandkids, but she was glad to help whenever she could. As she parked, she saw that the tulips Sara had planted were in full bloom, brightening up the boxes in front of the house. She knocked and then heard scurrying feet and shrieks from inside.

"Grandma!" four-year-old Aiden shouted, throwing the door open.

"You don't open the door, Aiden," Sara called from the kitchen.

"But it's not a stranger. It's Grandma," Aiden argued.

"But you didn't know it was Grandma," Sara said as she strode toward the door. Her hair was curled, and she wore a pretty blue dress. "Hi, Mom. Thanks so much for coming."

"Of course." Tracy gave Aiden a big hug. "Your mom is right, you know. You should let grown-ups answer the door."

"Okay, Grandma. Come see my trains."

Tracy let Aiden pull her into the living room, where he'd set up an elaborate wooden train track. Two-year-old Zoe was watching a cartoon but squealed with delight when she saw Tracy. "Gamma!"

Sarah finished getting ready to go, and then called, "Thanks, Mom," before hurrying out the door to meet Kevin.

Tracy spent the next hour feeding her grandkids mac and cheese with hot dogs then gave them baths before snuggling down on the couch to read with them. After she prayed with them and tucked them into bed, Tracy headed back out to the living room. She tidied the kitchen and folded the load of clean clothes that sat in the laundry basket, and then she looked around, trying to decide what to do. She could watch TV or she could read the book she'd brought with her. But what she really wanted to do was check her email and see if Ruben from Sandwich had sent her the information from the auction sale.

She sat on the couch and got out her phone. Ruben had forwarded the confirmation that he'd purchased the laptop as well as another email with a tracking number.

The first email featured a small image of the item's original listing on the auction site along with the agreed-upon price. It was far less than she would have expected to pay for a laptop. The seller's name was ExploreByDay, and their location was listed as Springfield, Illinois. Springfield? So someone from the dinner had stolen the laptop and then driven to their hideout in Springfield to sell the stolen goods?

Okay, maybe not a hideout. And at least that explained why her laptop hadn't come up on the auction sites. She'd kept her searches local. She supposed that was shortsighted when it was possible to drive to another state in a matter of hours, but at the same time, she couldn't exactly have combed through all the laptops in a hundred-and-fifty-mile radius. And it didn't matter anyway. They knew where her laptop was, and hopefully whoever ExploreByDay was also had Jeff's laptop, or knew where it had gone. They still needed to find Anna's phone and ring light, but hopefully ExploreByDay knew where those were as well.

The problem was that she had no clue who ExploreByDay was. Could she figure out where in Springfield they were? There must be some account registration information somewhere. Surely ExploreByDay had registered for the auction site using a real name and address. Would she be able to access that information? She doubted it. Dale should be able to get the site to share their records once it was reported that the seller had sold stolen items. But even if he could, would it lead to real information about the seller? Someone had used a fake ID to pawn the jewelry. If it was the same person, Tracy didn't think it was likely they would use their real name online, where it was so much easier to hide.

Tracy closed the receipt email and opened the other one, which showed the tracking information for the shipment of the laptop. She clicked on the tracking number, and it took her to the shipping company's website. Tracy had seen pages like it plenty of times. It allowed a viewer to see when a package was shipped, when it reached a distribution point, and when it was out for delivery. She studied the information for the laptop. It had been shipped on Tuesday and reached Massachusetts on Thursday. It was delivered that morning and signed for by Ruben Carter. She read the page again, confirming that the laptop had been shipped Tuesday from—

Wait a minute.

She checked the first email again. Sure enough, the seller had reported that the package was shipped from Springfield, Illinois.

But actually, according to the tracking information, the package hadn't been shipped from Illinois at all. It had been shipped from La Grange, Missouri.

Whoever shipped that laptop had done it from right here, in a town ten minutes away from Canton.

In other words, the thief hadn't taken the stolen laptop very far before selling it. They were in La Grange, or had been three days ago.

The thief might still have the other missing laptop and items with them in La Grange. Did that mean that the address on the fake ID might not have been so fake? Was the blond woman from La Grange?

It couldn't be that hard to track down the exact place the laptop was shipped from. La Grange was a small town. How many shipping locations could there be? A quick search revealed exactly one—a copy and print store called PrintIt Copy and Office Supplies. It looked like a mom-and-pop shop. Maybe whoever was on duty there when the laptop was mailed would be able to tell her about the seller. She would make a trip to La Grange as soon as she could.

The thief was close. Now if only she could figure out who ExploreByDay was.

She was getting closer. She could feel it.

Chapter Nineteen

Saturday morning, Robin picked Tracy up around nine as promised, and Tracy climbed into her cousin's car, travel mug of coffee in hand.

"So tell me what you know about this dealer," Tracy said as Robin drove through the streets of Canton. They passed Jody's pink house, and Tracy found herself wondering once again if Jody was involved with the thefts in any way.

"His name's Clyde Fletcher. He's been in the antiques business forever. Probably forty years or so, if I had to guess."

"So he knows a lot of other dealers."

"Right. His specialty is jewelry and watches, and he knows pretty much everyone who sells such things. I ran across him in an online forum for professionals in the industry. He's great about answering questions for other sellers and dealers. I finally met him in person at a convention about five years ago."

"I can't even imagine what a convention of antiques dealers must be like."

"Probably a lot like Jeff's faculty dinners, if I had to guess," Robin said. "Lots of history buffs come together and talk ad nauseam about the minutiae of things the rest of the world has moved on from."

"That sounds about right." Tracy chuckled as they left the downtown area and made for the highway.

"Anyway, like I said, I met him at this convention. I went up to talk to him after he gave a workshop about Victorian mourning jewelry."

"About what?"

"Mourning jewelry. You've never heard of it?"

Tracy raised an eyebrow, and Robin laughed. "You're right. Silly question. It was very popular in the Georgian and Victorian eras. Mourning pieces were usually made from jet or other dark stones, and some of the earlier pieces feature macabre images of coffins, tombstones, or even skulls—things like that."

"Why in the world would anyone want to wear jewelry with a coffin on it?" Tracy asked, aghast.

"It was meant to be a *memento mori*—which roughly translates to 'Remember you must die.' It was a reminder that death would come for all of us someday."

Tracy shuddered. "Who wants to be reminded of that?"

"I don't know. I think a reminder that this life is not all there is can be encouraging, actually. Remembering our own mortality is important."

"Okay," Tracy said. "I guess I can see that, but it doesn't mean I want to wear a ring with a tombstone on it."

"Maybe you'd be more into hair?"

"Hair?"

"In the Victorian era, mourning jewelry was less about death in general and more about commemorating the loss of a loved one. Sometimes the pieces were engraved with dates and names, and sometimes they even included hair from the loved one, either braided or worked into the design somehow."

Tracy couldn't keep from making a face. "No thank you."

"Mourning jewelry fell out of fashion, obviously. But as you can see, there are all kinds of interesting things you can learn at an antiques convention. Clyde's lecture was absolutely fascinating. My hand cramped from writing notes."

"I'm glad you were able to enjoy it." As much as Tracy loved antiques, mourning jewelry sounded a bit too gruesome for her taste. "Anyway, you were able to meet Clyde after the lecture?"

"Yes. And he was so nice and encouraging, even though he's one of the biggest experts in his field. We've kept in touch over the years, and he's helped me find buyers for some of my pieces. I found this gorgeous cameo at an estate sale a couple of years ago, and he helped connect me with a collector."

"He sounds like a good guy to know."

"His real passion is watches, so I'm hopeful he'll be able to tell us something about Tom's watch."

"After we drive all this way, I hope so too," Tracy said. The highway flew past, largely empty on a Saturday morning.

"We should be there in about twenty minutes," Robin said.

Hannibal was a historic river town with a stretch of classic brick buildings downtown, but it was clear as soon as they entered the outskirts who its most famous resident was. There were signs for Mark Twain's boyhood home, murals and statues featuring the famous author, and even signs pointing to Tom Sawyer's fence and the cave that had inspired the fictional character's adventures. Lots of people were out walking on the beautiful spring morning, and some were even dressed in period costume.

"Clyde's shop is right up there," Robin said as she pulled into a parking spot along the downtown strip.

They strolled past several cute boutiques, a café, and a Mark Twain museum before stepping into a shop with big windows and a high pressed-tin ceiling. Though Clyde had a few furniture pieces and some decor items on display, much of the space was taken up by long glass cases featuring jewelry and watches from all different eras, according to the explanatory cards beside them.

"Good morning, Robin." A tall man with white hair came out of a back room carrying a tray of gleaming rings and necklaces. "You made it."

"Thanks so much for letting us come by." Robin gestured at Tracy. "This is my cousin Tracy."

"It's good to meet you," Tracy said.

Clyde set the tray on the glass case and came forward to shake her hand. "You as well. Now, are you the cousin who's in on the hunt for that missing Datejust?"

"I am," Tracy said.

"It's such a shame to lose a piece like that," Clyde said. "I'm sure there's great sentimental value as well, but aside from that, it's a beautiful watch. The Rolex Datejust is iconic."

"It is?" Tracy asked the question hesitantly, hoping she hadn't opened the door to a lecture about skulls and human hair.

"When the Datejust was first introduced in 1945 to celebrate Rolex's fortieth anniversary, it was the first self-winding wristwatch to display the date on its face, and it also featured a waterproof case the company had introduced nearly twenty years before."

Tracy thought it was fascinating that they'd made a waterproof watch a hundred years ago. She wanted him to elaborate on that point a bit, but Clyde continued before she could open her mouth.

"That first model, the 4467, is highly valued by collectors today. Another popular one is the 1953 model, where they introduced the Cyclops lens, which is that bubble over the date that magnifies it for easier reading," he said. "That was a true innovation and has become an iconic symbol of the Datejust, and Rolex itself."

"I had no idea." Tracy could see that he really knew his antique watches and truly loved them.

"Now, the watch you're missing is the 1955 model, right?" Clyde went around behind the glass display case and used a key to open it. Then he began setting the jewelry from the tray inside.

"That's right," Robin said. "Have you seen it?"

"It's hard to say for sure," Clyde said. "But every Rolex is engraved with a serial number. Do you know the number of yours?"

"Yes." Robin pulled out the paperwork they'd found in the attic. "I have it here."

"Perfect." Clyde smiled at her. "Give me a minute, and I'll go check my records." He took the papers and went through the door behind the counter.

While he was gone, Tracy and Robin browsed his wares. There were a lot of watches available, and Tracy imagined a collector must know the differences between them, but she couldn't hazard a guess as to what made each one special. Still, there were some attractive ones. She really liked one with a simple gold band and a pearlized blue face.

A Thief in the Night

Eventually, Clyde reemerged. "I'm afraid I haven't seen this watch in here," he said. "But I reached out to a friend of mine from St. Louis after you contacted me. His name is Malcolm Foxworth. He told me he has a record of selling a Datejust matching the exact specifications as yours about a year ago."

"Can we talk to him?" Tracy asked.

"Where is the watch now?" Robin asked at the same time.

Clyde laughed. "He's away on a buying trip to Venice, and he's not answering his phone right now. Fortunately, he keeps meticulous records, and he was able to find the name of the person who sold him the watch. It's someone he's bought multiple pieces from over the past year or so. Not someone in the trade, as far as he knows. She simply seems to have an interest in jewelry and watches. Her name is Liz Chapin."

Tracy grabbed a notebook from her purse and jotted down the name.

"She's from Kansas City," Clyde said. "He tells me he's bought a few watches and half a dozen pieces of jewelry from her. He couldn't tell me anything more about her, I'm afraid. I'm sure he has the name of the person who bought it from him too, though he didn't tell me that information."

Was there any chance that Liz Chapin was the blond woman who was going by Melissa Hogarth? But if she was, wouldn't she have used her fake ID and name to sell the jewelry to Malcolm?

"Now that I have that serial number, I'll send it to him and see if he can find it in his records. He'll get back to me when he can. It will probably be a bit delayed though. From what I understand, he's busy eating pasta and drinking cappuccinos while squeezing in some antique collecting when he can."

"Venice sounds lovely." Tracy had never been to Italy, but she'd seen photos of the narrow lanes, the bridges over the canals, and the gondoliers who ferried riders through the enchanting city. She hoped to make it there someday, and for more than the cappuccinos and pasta.

"It is," Clyde said. "And there are lots of antiques there, though honestly I think he simply loves an excuse to go to Italy."

"Sign me up," Robin said. "I want an excuse to go too."

"You and me both," Clyde said.

"If he could track down the name of the person who bought the watch, that would be helpful," Robin said.

"I'll ask him about that too," Clyde said. "I'm sure he'll respond to me as soon as he finishes his next gondola ride. He's also asked me to pass on his business card to you, so you can contact him directly if you'd like." He handed the card to Tracy, who thanked him and pocketed it.

"How rare are these particular watches?" Robin asked.

"Rare enough that Malcolm remembered it," Clyde said. "We see plenty of Rolexes. They're highly collectible because the brand name has so much prestige. But it's rare to find one that old, and the Datejust is such a classic watch that there's always a market for them. If you come across one from the fifties in good shape, you're pretty much guaranteed to find a buyer and get a good price. Which is no doubt why someone recognized the opportunity when they came across the piece."

But who had known about it? Tracy wondered if there was any way Tom would have been the one to sell the watch to Liz Chapin, and whether he would have collected insurance money for it. It was so far-fetched. But since he'd had the watch appraised, he knew exactly how valuable it was.

Well, Tracy was certain of one thing. She had a new lead, and her next step was to dig into the name Liz Chapin.

"We really appreciate your help," Tracy said.

"Anytime." Clyde waved, and they headed back out onto the street.

On their way to the car, they spotted a French bakery that displayed alluring pastries in the window, so Robin suggested they stop in and get some sustenance for the journey home.

A few minutes later, Tracy had polished off the best croissant she'd ever eaten, Robin had consumed an éclair, and they were on the road.

As Robin drove, Tracy used her phone to do some research. "There's a high school track star by the name of Liz Chapin in Fremont, California," she reported, squinting at her phone.

"That's probably not the one we need." Robin kept her eyes on the road as she drove. "What else?"

"There's a botanist in Yorkshire, England, by that name. She's probably in her sixties or so, judging by this photo."

"Unlikely to be the right one."

"I agree." Tracy scrolled down lower on the page. "Let's see. I found a video channel for someone named Lizzie Chapin. She makes videos about cake decorating. I think she's probably in her twenties. She makes some cool cakes—here's a dinosaur, and one that resembles a rocket ship, and this one's a cat."

"I think I would enjoy watching those videos, but, sadly, I don't think that's our girl."

"I think you're right."

Tracy kept scrolling, and she was about to give up when something caught her eye. "Hang on."

"I'm driving sixty-five miles an hour. I'm not going anywhere."

Tracy ignored her cousin's joke and stared at the screen, reading the article carefully. Then she examined the photo again. "I think I've found something."

Chapter Twenty

As they continued the drive home, Tracy did some more digging around online to make sure she was right about Liz Chapin. After checking the archives of the *Kansas City Star* as well as the white pages for the area, Tracy was pretty sure she'd figured out who the mysterious watch and jewelry collector was.

But before they did anything about it, Tracy wanted to gather as much data as she could, so she sent an email to Clyde's friend Malcolm, asking for more information about the items he'd purchased from Liz Chapin.

Tracy sat in her seat and reflected. She had a lead on the watch, and as of last night, she knew where her laptop was and where it had been mailed to Massachusetts from.

"Want to make a stop before we head back?" Tracy asked.

"Sure. Millie and Hayley are opening the store today, so I've got a bit of time. They can handle things for a little while longer," Robin said. "What did you have in mind?"

"It's on our way home. There's a shipping location in La Grange I'd like to stop by."

"Weird, but okay. I'm game."

"It's the place my laptop was mailed from," Tracy said. "I'm hoping they might be able to tell me something about the person who sent it."

"How did you manage to find out where your laptop was mailed from?" Robin asked, her eyebrows practically to her hairline.

Tracy explained as she routed the GPS to PrintIt, and they found the place easily enough. It was in a row of businesses in a generic shopping center with a terra-cotta tile roof. Inside they found a neutral space lined with slatwall. Large photocopiers took up much of the floor space, and displays of padded mailing envelopes and bubble wrap decorated the walls.

A woman with gray hair stood behind the counter. "Hello. Can I help you?"

"Hi." Tracy put on her most winning smile. "I'm hoping you can help me with something. A package was mailed from this location on Tuesday, and I'm trying to learn about the person who mailed it."

"Shipped." The woman's voice was clipped.

"What?"

"You *mail* a letter. You *ship* a package."

Tracy glanced at Robin, who was clearly trying to hide a grin. "I see. Thank you for letting me know. Is there anything you can tell me about the sender?"

"Are you the recipient of the package?"

"No, but—"

"Are you with the police?"

"No, I'm not a police officer."

"Then I'm afraid I can't help you. It's a matter of privacy, you see. We want to make sure our customers know that whatever they're shipping, it will not be made public."

"But the package contained something that belongs to me. I'm trying to find the person who took it."

"I'm sorry, but those are the rules." She didn't sound at all sorry. "The reason this shop is still in business after so many years is that our customers trust us to maintain their privacy."

Tracy couldn't help but think it had more to do with the fact that it was the *only* place in town to mail—wait, to *ship*—packages, but she didn't think it would help her cause to say that out loud.

"What about the security cameras?" Robin pointed to the cameras that were mounted in the corners of the room. "Is there any chance we could take a peek at the footage?"

"I'm afraid not," the woman said. "Not unless you're with the police and come with a warrant."

"Even when what was shipped from this location was stolen goods?"

"We are happy to work with the police on any matter. But I'm afraid I don't know you from Adam, and I can't go around sharing information about my customers with whoever walks in off the street."

Tracy wanted to argue, but she understood. She would make sure Dale visited PrintIt, if he hadn't yet, and hopefully the woman would give him the footage and cooperate with him.

In the car, Tracy said, "That was a wasted trip."

"Well, she had a point," Robin said as she put the car in gear. "I don't share information about a customer's purchase with whoever comes in asking about it."

"I guess you're right. But I'm calling Dale. It sounds like she would probably talk to him."

"I think that's a good idea."

When Tracy called Dale and told him where she'd been, he sighed. "Tracy, I will get to the bottom of this."

"I know, but I wasn't sure if you had discovered where the package was shipped from. And since the owner said she would talk to the police, I wanted to make sure I passed along what I found out. They had security cameras and everything, so it could be a lead, if not a full break in the case."

"I'll check it out," Dale promised. "Let's hope there are some identifying characteristics to help us figure out who it is."

Tracy knew that Dale was doing his best, but it had already been a week. In that time, her laptop had ended up on the East Coast and Melody's jewelry had been sold. There was no telling where the other missing items were. They could be on the other side of the world by now. Tracy was losing hope with each passing day that they would be recovered.

She was lucky she and Jeff had insurance that could replace the laptops if they didn't get them back, and Anna had already bought a new phone. All three of them had changed their banking and credit card passwords. Computers and phones were just things, she knew that. But it was a matter of principle. She didn't want to spend the rest of her life hesitant about inviting people over for dinner, afraid that perhaps something less easily replaceable would disappear. And she didn't want that for her fellow hosts either.

Chapter Twenty-One

Tracy checked her email Sunday morning before church and saw that she had gotten a reply from Malcolm the antiques dealer, who had added Clyde to the email so he would have the responses as well. She pumped her fist when she saw that Malcolm had included a full list of the items he had bought from Liz Chapin over the years.

In addition to the Rolex, Liz had sold Malcolm a 1962 Longine gold wristwatch, a two-carat emerald ring with a silver filigree setting, and a 1960s vintage Cartier diamond bracelet. He included photos of each item, and he confirmed that the serial number on the Rolex he'd sold matched the serial number of Tom's watch. He admitted he didn't always ask about each item's provenance but would be very interested to learn if they came from unseemly sources. He also told her that he'd met Liz Chapin, and from the description he gave, Tracy knew she had indeed figured out who Liz was.

Tracy decided she would go find Liz after church and see if she could get the watch issue solved once and for all. The first thing she did was text Robin. HEARD FROM MALCOLM.

It took only a moment for Robin to reply. IS IT TOM'S WATCH?

IT IS! AND I KNOW FOR SURE WHO LIZ CHAPIN IS. WANT TO GO CATCH A THIEF AFTER CHURCH?

Robin sent a thumbs-up, and Tracy printed out the report of items Malcolm had sent her, grateful she could use her printer from her phone. Then she made buttermilk pancakes and bacon, and she and Jeff drank coffee and talked about their week. She made sure the chicken for the evening's family dinner had thawed after a stint in the freezer, and then she got ready for church.

As usual, the stress and confusion of the week melted away as soon as the church service began, with the hymn "O For a Thousand Tongues to Sing." The wondering, the suspicion, the fear—none of that really mattered, in the grand scheme of things. The laptop and the phone and the watch were simply things. They were not what gave life meaning.

"O, for a thousand tongues to sing my great Redeemer's praise," the congregation sang. "The glories of my God and King, the triumphs of His grace." Tracy would never get tired of singing praise to the one true God and King.

She also enjoyed Pastor Gary's sermon about the passage in Luke when the resurrected Christ appeared to the disciples on the road to Emmaus and they didn't recognize Him. These were people who had been with Jesus during His ministry. They had eaten with Him and camped with Him and seen Him perform miracles. And yet, because they had seen Him crucified and laid in a tomb, they didn't believe it was Jesus who walked with them. They were so convinced Jesus was dead that they completely missed the fact that they were talking to the One death had no hold over. They missed what was right in front of them because it wasn't what they had expected to see.

How many times had Tracy missed glimpsing Jesus because she didn't understand the ways God was trying to teach her? How many times had she missed what was right in front of her because it wasn't what she expected to see?

As they sang the final hymn, she gazed around the congregation and saw many of the people she had talked to in the past week. There were Tom and Angie, set to head home for Lincoln in the morning. They were sitting with Angie's parents. Jody Bonilla wore a perfectly tailored floral sheath dress, without a hair out of place. She stood in sharp contrast to her daughter, Louisa, in baggy jeans, combat boots, and an oversized sweater. There were Sharon and Caleb, and Jeannie with her mom and the kids. Robert West was with his wife, and Bethany Hill sat with a group of twentysomethings.

Millie Ettlinger sat next her daughter, Dottie, though Arielle wasn't there. Had she gone home? She had never returned Tracy's calls or texts, and Tracy hadn't seen her since the night of the party. She was starting to get a really bad feeling about that. Hadn't Millie said that Arielle was still around? She wouldn't lie about that, would she? But why didn't Arielle respond to her? Tracy didn't like that. She would try to find Millie after the service and see if she could get answers.

So many members of her own family were present as well. Amy and Miles with their four kids. Anna and Chad, and Sara and Kevin and all the grandkids. Aunt Ruth and Uncle Marvin shared a pew with Robin and her family. And Jeff stood at Tracy's side, handsome as ever in his blue button-down. Tracy was blessed to be able to spend so much time with the people she loved.

When the service ended, Tracy slowly made her way to coffee hour, greeting several familiar faces along the way. When she reached the fellowship hall, the first person she saw was Jody. The single mom stood by the hospitality table, clutching a cup of coffee and hissing something under her breath at Louisa, who seemed like she wanted to be anywhere else. Louisa's hair was cut short, and the light brown tips held the faintest remains of what might have been blue hair dye.

The moment Jody saw Tracy enter the room, her face changed, and she quickly plastered a smile onto her face. "Hi, Tracy. How are you? How was your week?"

If Tracy hadn't seen her so visibly upset with Louisa a moment before, she would have thought there was nothing wrong. It was as if that Jody vanished before Tracy's eyes and a cheerful, happy Jody had taken her place. It was unsettling, truthfully.

"It was—it was strange," Tracy admitted. Maybe if she didn't try to act like everything was perfect, Jody would feel free to do the same. "Honestly, much of it was spent dealing with the missing laptops and whatnot from last Saturday."

"Have they still not found out who was behind that?" Jody's eyes widened. "I was sure the police would have caught the thief by now."

"I'm afraid not." Tracy turned to Louisa, who had already rolled her eyes twice during the exchange. "And you must be Louisa. It's so nice to meet you."

"Hey," the teenager mumbled.

"Lou, this is Tracy. She was one of the hosts of the progressive dinner last weekend."

"Cool." She gestured with her head. "I'm gonna go sit over there."

"Okay." Jody's tone indicated that she wished Louisa wouldn't, but the girl either didn't understand or—more likely—ignored it. She stalked away, her ripped jeans brushing the floor with each step.

"How are you? Did you have a good week?" Tracy asked.

"It was great. We're settling into our new home and loving every second."

Tracy didn't buy it. Not at all. Jody's tone was too chipper, too eager. She was trying too hard, as Tracy and Amy had suspected.

"You start your new job this week, right?"

"Tomorrow. I will admit to some first-day jitters, but mostly I'm excited."

"And how's Louisa settling in?" Tracy glanced over at the girl, who had taken a seat in one of the folding chairs lining the wall of the fellowship hall and was scrolling on her phone.

Wait. That phone case sure looked a lot like Anna's. It had the same white-and-gold pattern. The phone was about the same size as Anna's as well, though those phones were so common, it was hard to say for sure. But Tracy was almost sure that was the same case Anna had had on her phone.

But surely that wasn't Anna's phone. Even if Louisa had ended up with Anna's phone, would she be foolish enough to keep it in the same case and bring it to church, where it was sure to be spotted?

"She's doing all right," Jody said, her voice maintaining the same forced, chipper tone. "It's taking her a bit longer to settle in, but she'll get there."

"The teens are a tough age anyway," Tracy said. "And it can't be easy to move to a new town where everyone has known each other forever."

"She's okay," Jody said, though her voice had lost its bravado.

"When we spoke a few days ago, you said she was having a pretty tough time," Tracy said.

Jody pressed her lips together into a thin line.

"It can be hard to see your child struggling," Tracy said. "For a while when my son was in high school, he was bullied, and I think it might have been the hardest thing I ever went through as a mom. He was smaller than a lot of the other boys, he was into marching band and science, and some of the other kids apparently saw him as an easy target. We got through it. He hit a growth spurt his sophomore year and eventually made some good friends. But for a while there, he really struggled, and it was so hard as a mom to try to figure out how to help him. When your kid is in pain, it eats you up inside."

Jody was still pressing her lips together, and the determinedly cheerful expression on her face had vanished. It almost seemed as if she held back tears.

"You've both been through a lot," Tracy said gently. She sensed that whatever dam held Jody's real feelings in check was about to crack, to allow her true feelings to burst through. "But you're doing so well now."

Tears spilled down Jody's cheeks. "That's the thing," she sobbed. Then she sucked in a long breath, trying to calm herself. "We're not doing well. Not really. I know it may appear that way, but it's not true."

Tracy slid her arm around Jody's shoulders and led her to a quiet corner of the room. She pulled a pack of tissues from her purse and handed one to Jody, who took it and wiped her eyes.

"The divorce is dragging out way longer than it needs to," she went on. "My ex is being so nasty, fighting over every little thing. He doesn't want me to have Louisa or any of our money. His money,

A Thief in the Night

he calls it. He already got the house, the retirement accounts, everything. He's left us with nothing. We had to move to this little town because it was the best job offer I got, and Louisa hates me for it."

Tracy tried to ignore the dig at her hometown. It wasn't everyone's idea of paradise, though it was hers. She tried to focus on what Jody was saying instead. "That's terrible. How can he get away with that?"

"I signed a prenup," Jody said. "Stupidly. There was so much I didn't understand back then. And now I'm barely getting by while he's got everything, and it's just—it's so hard, you know?"

"I can only imagine," Tracy said. "Of course it's hard."

"We're used to living a certain way, and I guess I got comfortable. And now I can't stop acting like nothing has changed, even though I can't afford that lifestyle anymore. The high-end brands and fancy things bring me comfort and make me feel like things are the way they used to be, even though that couldn't be further from the truth. I've been so stupid."

"You've been doing what has helped you make it through a tough time," Tracy said kindly. Listening to Jody, she couldn't help but be moved. The woman was suffering, and she was doing it alone.

"I'm in so much credit card debt," Jody said. "But I can't make myself stop. It's like I need to have the right stuff to show the world I'm doing okay—to show my ex that I'm doing okay—but I'm not, and it's making everything worse."

"I'm so sorry." Tracy truly did feel for her. She had never been one for labels and shopping, personally, but did she still care more than she should about how the rest of the world saw her? Tracy didn't want to admit it, even to herself, but she sometimes let the opinions of others influence her. And she hadn't dealt with the major upheaval and trauma Jody had.

"Louisa knows how guilty I feel about all of it. She's been milking it for all it's worth, asking me for the latest phone, the latest computer, all that. Like a fool, I give in, because even though I know money can't buy happiness, when it comes to my kid, I'm willing to try. I'm willing to do anything if it will help make this all easier on her."

"That's totally understandable," Tracy said. Her mind raced. This was the opportunity she needed. How could she make her next question sound natural? "I see she has a nice new phone. Is that part of it all?"

"Yes," Jody said. "She absolutely had to have it to keep in touch with her friends back home. A new laptop too. Do you know how much those things cost?"

"I do," Tracy said nodding.

"Of course you do," Jody said, shaking her head. "Obviously. Anyway, I recognized how nice Jeff's laptop was because I'd recently bought the same model for Louisa. Not that she ever thanked me, of course."

"So both her phone and her laptop are things you recently bought her?" Tracy confirmed.

"That's right. I can show you the receipts if you want. I know you wondered, and I can't blame you, but I promise I had nothing to do with the stolen laptops or phone. Why would I steal them, when I can use my platinum card to dig myself deeper into a financial hole?" She gave a laugh, but it sounded sad.

Tracy believed her, and not only because of the tears. What convinced Tracy was that Jody's logic, as twisted and bizarre as it was, made sense. Jody was used to buying what she wanted. If she wanted a new phone or laptop for her daughter, she would buy it out of pride if not wisdom. She hadn't stolen the laptops that night.

But if she hadn't, who had?

Tracy put the question to the back of her mind and sat with Jody until her tears dried.

Finally, Jody sniffled and gave her a watery smile. "I'm so sorry to unload all of this on you,"

"I'm grateful you trusted me enough to share," Tracy said. "You don't have to go through this alone, by the way. Pastor Gary offers counseling to his congregation. I'm sure he'd be happy to meet with you."

"That might be nice," Jody said. "That's probably a good idea, actually."

"Do you have his contact information?" Tracy asked.

"I've seen it in the bulletin," Jody said.

"I think it would be a good idea for you to connect with him," Tracy said. "Though I hope you and I can also keep talking."

Jody wiped her nose. "Thank you, Tracy."

Tracy gave Jody a hug and promised to check in with her, and then Jody gathered up a sullen Louisa and ushered her out the door.

Tracy scanned the room and was glad to see that Millie hadn't left yet. She was chatting with Kathy, Pastor Gary's wife, while Dottie played some kind of game with Miles and Amy's daughters, Jana and Natalie.

Tracy made her way across the room and smiled as she joined Millie and Kathy. Kathy returned the greeting, but Millie's face froze when she saw Tracy.

"Hi, Millie, Kathy. How are you both?" Tracy asked.

"Hi, Tracy," Kathy said. "We were just chatting about the Memorial Day picnic."

"How can it be time to start thinking about Memorial Day already? It's barely past Easter."

Kathy chuckled. "It's crazy, isn't it? But it's already just a little over a month away, if you can believe it. Millie volunteered to head up the potluck."

"I know a thing or two about feeding lots of people," Millie said, referring to her part-time job working in the high school cafeteria.

"That's great." Tracy realized the conversation had given her the opening she needed. "I can't wait. Will Arielle be able to make it to the picnic?"

Millie bit her lip. "No, I don't think she will."

"Is she still in town? Or did she go home?" Tracy asked. "I haven't seen her around, and she still hasn't returned my calls or texts."

"She's very busy," Millie said. "I'm sure she'll get back to you soon though." But her tone told Tracy that Millie didn't believe her own words.

Tracy didn't want to badger her friend, but she couldn't let it go. She suspected that Millie didn't know where Arielle was any more than Tracy did. She hadn't been able to get her sister to text Tracy back, because Arielle was long gone from Canton. Had she taken the laptops and phone with her? Arielle had dark hair, so she wasn't an obvious suspect for Melissa Hogarth, but she could have worn a wig. She was one of the few suspects left.

Tracy decided to push a bit more. "Where does Arielle live? I've forgotten where you said she was visiting from."

"St. Louis," Millie said. "She's lived there since she moved there for college."

"And how often does she come to visit?" Tracy asked.

"Every so often." Millie shifted her weight from one foot to the other. "Not regularly, but sometimes."

"She doesn't seem to still be around. Did she go back to St. Louis?" Tracy asked.

Millie didn't answer for a moment, and her gaze darted from one corner of the room to another. Then she blurted, "I'm sorry, Tracy, but I have to get Dottie home for lunch. Mom and Dad are probably waiting for us."

She bolted. Tracy watched her scoop up Dottie—who loudly protested being separated from her friends—before heading up the stairs and disappearing.

Tracy stood there, stunned. That interaction had been more than a little strange. Millie was covering up for her sister. Tracy was sure of it. Something was off, and Millie didn't want to admit it. Millie didn't know where Arielle was, and she was clearly worried about her sister, as well as Tracy's interest in her.

Arielle had been at the bottom of Tracy's suspect list, but now she'd worked herself directly to the top.

Tracy scanned the room until she spotted Robin, who caught her eye and raised her eyebrows. Tracy nodded. Robin excused herself from the conversation she was in, and Tracy went to find Jeff to let him know she was leaving with Robin. He planned to go for a bike ride that afternoon, and she promised to be home soon.

Tracy and Robin left the church and hurried to Robin's car. Tracy was still unsettled, her mind swirling as she filled Robin in on Malcolm's email and her odd conversation with Millie.

Tracy's spirits rose when Robin pulled up in front of Dimas Jewelers.

If she was right about Liz Chapin's real identity, they were finally about to find out what had really happened to Grandpa Howard's watch.

Chapter Twenty-Two

When Tracy and Robin walked into Dimas Jewelers, Simon stood behind the glass display case, helping a clearly nervous young man examine the diamond solitaires.

Robin and Tracy exchanged a smile.

"Do you know what cut she prefers?" Simon asked. "You can see we have several different styles here. This one is a brilliant cut—the round one. This one is a cushion cut, this is a pear-shape, and this is a princess cut." As he spoke, Simon pointed to different rings inside the display case.

"I don't know. I didn't know there were so many different kinds," the young man said.

"Tell me about your girlfriend. Is she traditional? Or does she like things that are a little more modern?" Simon asked.

"I think modern," he said, though he sounded uncertain.

"I might suggest a princess cut or a cushion cut in that case," Simon said. "Once we narrow down the cut, we can think about carat—that's size—and the clarity and color."

"Um, diamond-colored," the guy said helplessly.

"Why don't you browse for a minute and see if any of the rings on display remind you of ones you've seen your girlfriend wear," Simon suggested. Tracy imagined he must have had the same conversation hundreds of times in his career, and it was clear he was good at helping clueless boyfriends make one of the most significant purchases of their lives.

"The most important thing to remember is that it's not about the ring, it's about you. She'll say yes or no because of who *you* are, not because of the ring itself."

"But I want to get her one she likes," the young man protested.

"I'm sure she will like any of these," Simon said. "And if it's not exactly what she was hoping for, you can always come in together and exchange it."

Relief washed over the young man's face. "Okay. Thank you."

Simon left him to peruse the selection in the case and walked over to where Tracy and Robin waited. Tracy didn't see any sign of the shop assistant. Elle, he'd called her. Well, now Tracy knew what that was short for.

He pushed his bifocals up on his head as he greeted them. "Any luck finding that watch?"

"Maybe," Tracy said. "Actually, that's what we wanted to talk to you about."

"Sure. How can I help?"

He appeared so open, so optimistic, so ready to help, that Tracy felt terrible for what they were about to tell him.

"I reached out to some of my connections," Robin said carefully. "On the off chance anyone remembered seeing a watch that matched the description of the one we're searching for."

"That's a great idea," Simon said. "Did something turn up?"

"It sure did. We spoke with a friend of mine. He focuses on antique watches and jewelry. He has a shop in Hannibal."

"Was it Clyde Fletcher, by any chance?"

"That's right."

Simon's face broke into a smile. "I know Clyde. Good guy. He knows his stuff."

"He does," Robin said. She paused. "He reached out to some of his connections, and he put us in contact with a dealer in St. Louis who remembered selling a 1955 Datejust about a year ago."

"Was it your grandfather's watch?" Simon asked eagerly.

"Yes, it was," Robin said.

"Well, are you going to leave me in suspense?" It was abundantly clear that Simon truly had no idea.

Tracy had no choice but to tell him. "The dealer bought the watch from someone named Liz Chapin."

Simon's mouth fell open. "That can't be right."

"I'm afraid it is," Tracy said gently. "He keeps very good records, and when I asked, he described her to me. Dark curly hair, blue eyes, tall. I'm afraid it's your niece, Eliza."

"We didn't make the connection at first. When we were here before, we heard you call her Elle," Robin said. "It wasn't until Tracy found her wedding announcement in the *Kansas City Star* that we put it together."

Tracy took out her phone and showed him the wedding announcement, which she'd pulled up. "'Eliza Barrett Chapin married Scott Erickson Fulton,'" Tracy read. She used two fingers to enlarge the image so Simon could see the wedding photo. Eliza's dark hair and pale skin were unmistakable, even in the grainy black-and-white photo.

"But that's impossible," Simon protested. "She would never do that to me. And even if she would, there's no way she could have. I have so much security in place."

Tracy remained quiet, letting him process the flood of emotions she could see washing over him.

Finally, he said, "When was this sale?"

"It was January of last year," Robin said. "Tom brought in the watch for a new battery when he visited at Christmas. We think that must have been when she swapped the original watch out for the fake then sold the original."

"She started working with me the previous fall," Simon said, sounding miserable. "Only a few months before that."

"And Tom left the watch here for a couple of days," Robin said. "He dropped it off the day before Christmas, and picked it up a day or two after the holiday."

"That would have given Eliza time to find a replacement," Tracy said.

"But why would she do that?" Simon argued. "Elle doesn't know anything about valuable jewelry. After she got married, she quit her job in Kansas City and moved here because her husband works at the college. She didn't have anything to do. So I hired her to help me clean and wait on customers. She doesn't know the first thing about antique watches, or how to sell them, or how to get a high-quality fake watch to replace one if you steal it."

"I'm afraid she's not as clueless as she's made you believe," Robin said. "When we were in here the other day, she sure knew a lot about these gemstones. She must have learned by working here."

"And if she learned about jewels, it stands to reason that she would have learned about watches as well," Tracy said. "Is it possible she overheard you talking with Tom about the watch while he was in the shop?"

"Yes. I suppose it's possible," he admitted. "She's very smart. I should have known she would pick things up quickly." He massaged his temples. "And now that I think about it, she has been incredibly helpful about greeting customers who come to pick up their items. Sometimes she whisks them away before I can get to them."

"Did she ever seem to suddenly have more cash than you would expect?" Robin asked.

"I don't know." Simon sounded defeated. "They're saving for a down payment. They don't spend a lot, so I wouldn't have noticed." He shook his head, as if he had trouble making sense of it.

Tracy couldn't imagine how he felt.

"But okay, let's say she did take the original," Simon said. "She had to replace it with a decent fake. How would she know where to get one of those?"

"I imagine the same way she knew where to find a dealer who would be interested in reselling it," Tracy said. "She did some research. We did a bit, and it's not that difficult to find reproductions of the real thing online."

"There are actually tons of sites on the internet that sell knock-off watches, purses, and accessories," Robin said. "It's a very lucrative business. It's totally illegal of course, but if you know where to find them, it's possible to get a high-quality watch—or at least one that passes for a high-quality watch to the untrained eye—at a fraction of the price you'd pay for the real thing."

"Tom's was good enough to pass for real for over a year," Tracy said. "At least until someone who knew what to look for spotted the problems with it."

Simon was silent for a moment. Then he said, "Are you positive? There can be no doubt?"

"Malcolm Foxworth, the dealer, gave us a list of items he bought from Eliza." Tracy tugged the printout from her purse and slid it across the counter to him. She was glad she'd brought it, but she also knew it would remove his protective layer of denial. She had a feeling she knew exactly where Eliza had gotten the pieces Malcolm had bought from her.

Simon ran one finger down the page, examining each item. His expression grew more and more dismayed. "He got all of these from Elle?"

"Do you recognize them?" Robin asked.

"They're all valuable pieces that have come into the shop in the past year or so," he said. "She knew exactly what she was doing. No one else could have done this. My own niece has been stealing from my customers, from me. How will anyone be able to trust my business again?"

"I'm sorry," Tracy said. The situation had to be so hard on him. Not only had he found out he'd been burgled multiple times, but his niece was behind it. And now the reputation of his family business was about to be damaged, possibly irrevocably.

"I'm not sure what to do now." His eyes brimmed with tears. "I'll have to fire her, naturally. That will happen right away. But I need to return the originals to their owners. How do I do that?"

"I'm afraid you'll probably need to get the police involved," Tracy said. "If you file a report, that will allow them to help you get the items returned."

"I can't call the police on Elle," Simon said. "She's my niece."

"I know she is," Tracy said. "But she's also responsible for stealing from your customers. Given the value of the items she stole, she'll probably be charged with multiple felonies. You don't want to be held accountable for what she's done or become an accessory."

"The police will help you," Robin said. "She stole from your customers, but she also stole from you. The police will understand that you're a victim, not an accomplice."

"I also think it's probably a good idea for you to contact Malcolm," Tracy said. "He'll be able to tell you who bought the originals. Once they're reported stolen, he'll work with you to get them back to the original owners. After all, he feels partially responsible, since he didn't ask enough questions about where she got the items."

"It's so hard to believe that someone I love—someone I trusted—could do something like this," Simon said.

Tracy understood how he must feel. When they had first started looking at suspects in the progressive dinner thefts, she had immediately discounted the possibility that anyone in her family could be involved. Amy, Sara, Susan and David, and Aunt Ruth and Uncle Marvin were all in the clear because she couldn't comprehend the possibility that someone she loved had stolen from her. And after she began to suspect Tom and Angie were hiding something from her, it was still hard to accept that Tom might have been responsible for selling the watch. Even now, though she still had no idea what was going on with them, Tracy couldn't quite bring herself to list them as suspects.

Simon gazed into the glass display case. Rubies, sapphires, and emeralds sparkled in the soft glow of the overhead light, next to pink topaz, amethyst, and garnet. The necklace Robin hoped to wear to a ball sparkled and twinkled at the edge of the display case. "Even if I'm not charged with anything, once the truth comes out, I could still lose all of this," he said quietly. "I could lose enough customers that I'll have to close. She risked everything my family—our family—has built over decades, all for some quick cash."

"I'm sorry," Robin murmured, laying a hand on his arm.

Finally, Simon lifted his chin. "I'll give Dale Leewright a call. I don't want to do it, but it's the right thing to do."

"I'm so sorry about this," Tracy said again. "Even though it's the right thing to do, it won't be easy."

"You have nothing to be sorry for. You found and told me the truth, and I know that was difficult for you," he said. "I'll get that watch back to you. I'll make sure your grandfather's Rolex gets returned. It's the least I can do after what my niece did to your family and so many others."

"Thank you," Robin murmured.

Suddenly, from the other side of the shop, someone said, "I think I want to go with the cushion one."

Tracy had forgotten the young man was still there. Judging by the way Robin and Simon startled at the sound of his voice, they had too.

Simon straightened and hurried around the display cases to meet him. "An excellent choice," he said, his usual charisma back in place. "She will cherish that ring, but more importantly, she will appreciate the care and thought you've put into this. It shows how much you love her."

The young man beamed at him.

Tracy wrote down Malcolm's contact information for Simon, and then she and Robin walked toward the door.

"I hope she says yes," Robin called as Tracy grabbed the door handle.

"I hope so too," the young man replied.

The cousins headed out, leaving Simon to help a customer choose the ring that would start a new family even as he mourned what he'd learned about his own.

Tracy wasn't sure what would happen with Eliza. She would likely be arrested and forced to make restitution for her crimes. It was hard to face the idea of a loved one committing such wrongs. Tracy knew it was right, but she also understood why Simon would want to protect his niece from all that, even when the evidence pointed her way. She knew herself well enough to realize that she would respond the exact same way in his shoes.

She thought about Tom and Angie and how strange they were acting.

Then she thought about Millie, about the mental hoops she'd jumped through to keep from admitting Arielle was gone, and how that made her look even more suspicious. Millie wanted to protect her sister, that was clear.

But it was time for the truth to come out there too, however painful it was.

Chapter Twenty-Three

When Tracy got home, Jeff was still out, and she knew she should get started on the main course for the family dinner. She was making fried chicken, and it took some prep time.

But the sight of Jeff's laptop on the kitchen table convinced her that first she should do a bit of research into Arielle.

Tracy grabbed a notebook and pen and logged on to Jeff's computer as Sadie settled at her feet. She started by listing everything she knew about Arielle. *Millie Ettlinger's sister*, she wrote at the top. *Younger, but how much? Lives in St. Louis.*

She tapped her pen on the table. She and Millie had worked together on a church service project a few years ago. While they'd packaged sandwiches for a local shelter, they'd gotten to talking, and Tracy was pretty sure Millie mentioned that her sister had run into some trouble over the years—getting in with the wrong crowd, falling behind on rent, various poor decisions. But that was a while ago. She could have turned her life around since then.

What did Arielle do for a living? Tracy couldn't remember any mention of it. She was pretty sure Arielle wasn't married, but didn't know if she had a boyfriend, or friends, or why she still lived in St. Louis and whether she liked it.

Tracy pulled up a search window. She couldn't think of Arielle's last name off the top of her head, but she knew it was on the list of names the church had sent the hosts before the progressive dinner. She found that and saw that Arielle's surname was Fleming. That sounded right. Somewhere Tracy had heard that Fleming was Millie's maiden name. She typed Arielle's full name into the search bar and scanned the results.

The first link was a social media page. Tracy clicked on it, and she saw that this was indeed the right Arielle. The page was littered with selfies of her—standing on a white sand beach in a bathing suit, in front of Big Ben, on the rim of the Grand Canyon, making faces in a bathroom mirror. She traveled a lot, if her page was to be believed. And she went to some incredible places, from what Tracy could tell. Her bio read, WANDERER. WONDERER. TRAVEL BLOGGER AND SEEKER.

Travel blogger. Huh. Nice work, if you can get it.

Tracy scrolled down and found that the travel posts had started about a year and a half ago. Before that, Arielle posted a lot of pictures of smoothies. What was that about? Tracy clicked on a few of the photos to read the captions and saw that Arielle had been selling protein powder. The smoothies were just a blip though—there were a lot of posts about them, but only over a period of about six months. Prior to that, there were several posts about a hair-care line and a few photos of Arielle in front of an office building in St. Louis. FIRST DAY AT THE NEW JOB, the caption read under one.

It was quite a career path. She moved from one thing to the next pretty quickly. Maybe she was finally happy with travel blogging though. It sounded like a pretty great career to Tracy, getting paid to see the world.

But it couldn't be the most stable. And it probably wasn't that lucrative, was it? Did Arielle make enough to support herself in St. Louis? Tracy scrolled to the top of the page and clicked on the first photo, the one of Arielle on a beach. Lovin' life in beautiful Belize, the caption read. Tracy didn't know anyone who had been to Belize. It looked amazing. But the photo was posted six months ago, back in November. Was it from Arielle's last trip? The others seemed to be closer together. Had she stopped traveling?

More importantly, where was she now?

Tracy scrolled, but she didn't find any more information about what Arielle was up to on the page, so she returned to the search page. She didn't find much. Arielle was quoted in an article in an independent newspaper in St. Louis, urging officials to cancel student debt. Tracy also discovered that she'd been a featured member of Washington University's track team a decade ago. That was it. Tracy found no indication about where Arielle was currently or what she was doing to make a living.

She sat back in her chair. There was nothing inherently suspicious about what she'd learned about Arielle. It was more that it didn't paint a picture of the most stable life, financial or otherwise.

Still, none of that proved she had anything to do with stealing the laptops, the jewelry, or the phone. None of it told her whether Arielle had been in La Grange to ship that laptop or whether she was ExploreByDay. Though honestly, ExploreByDay did sound like it could be a travel writer's name. Was there any way to find out if they were related?

Tracy went back to the social media page and noticed a link at the top. It went to a series of links, to the protein powder line, to the hair-care line, and—

The top link led to a blog called *Explore By Day, Write By Night*. Bingo.

Tracy clicked over to the blog that chronicled Arielle's journeys. She skimmed the first few entries, which described trips to an island off Puerto Rico, a forest of redwoods in California, and the Roman Colosseum. It sounded wonderful, but how in the world did Arielle afford such trips? Ads and links were all over the page, but she couldn't imagine they paid enough to fund so much travel. From what Tracy could tell, Arielle wasn't writing for a publication of any sort. But in any case, ExploreByDay had to be her.

Tracy reached for her phone so quickly she knocked it to the ground. Sadie stretched out and sniffed it before Tracy scooped it up and called Dale.

"Hi, Tracy." Dale sounded weary. He was probably getting sick of her calls. Plus, it was Sunday afternoon, and he was undoubtedly trying to relax with his family.

But this was important.

"Dale, have you been able to interview the shipping place in LaGrange? Did you see anyone on the security camera footage?"

"Tracy, number one, it's Sunday. Number two, we do have other cases we have to investigate. I know this case is important to you, but I can't give it my full attention all the time. So, no, I haven't been to LaGrange yet."

"I found the thief. I mean, I don't know where she is, but I know who she is. It's Millie's sister, Arielle Fleming. She's the one who stole the stuff from our houses."

"Slow down, Tracy. What happened?"

Tracy went back to the beginning, explaining how she'd tried to get in touch with Arielle several times in the past week, but Arielle never returned her calls, and—

"I spoke with her," Dale said. "I called her, and I was able to interview her."

"You were? How did you get her to talk with you?"

"I guess it's different when the police reach out to someone," Dale said dryly.

"Well, if you talked to her, then you know I'm right," Tracy said. "It was her."

"Actually, in my interview, she seemed very credible," Dale said. "She told me she hadn't seen anything and didn't know anything about the missing items until Millie told her about them after they got home from church the following day."

"But they weren't at church." Tracy's heart pounded. "Neither of them came to church the next day. She was lying."

"They weren't at church?" Dale sounded surprised by that.

"No," Tracy said. "I'm sure of it. I remember noticing their absence."

"Okay," Dale said. "But that doesn't mean it was her."

"Did you talk to her in person, or on the phone?" Tracy asked.

"The phone," Dale said. "She said she was watching Dottie for Millie and couldn't get away, but she was happy to talk over the phone."

"She didn't want to meet you in person because she wasn't in Canton," Tracy said. "She was—well, I don't know where, but she was in La Grange on Tuesday to send my laptop to Massachusetts."

"Hold on, Tracy." Dale cleared his throat. "That's quite an accusation. What brought you to that conclusion?"

Tracy explained how she'd grown more and more suspicious the longer it took for Arielle to call her back. She described finding Arielle's social media page and tracing her career trajectory to her travel blog. She related how the blog's title matched the handle of the seller who had listed Tracy's laptop on the auction site.

Dale asked her to repeat a few things, which told her he was taking notes. Relief flooded through her. He was taking her seriously.

"I don't know how I didn't see it before," Tracy said in conclusion. "She was so quiet Saturday night that I barely noticed her at all. She didn't say or do anything suspicious, unlike several of the other people there. I still have no idea how she got the items out of our homes. And she doesn't have blond hair, so I never suspected her of being Melissa Hogarth."

"We still don't know that she was the one with the fake ID," Dale reminded her.

"No, but it probably was," Tracy said. "She has dark hair, but she must have put on a wig for the picture."

"That's supposition."

"Well, if it wasn't her, it was someone working with her," Tracy said. "How else would 'Melissa Hogarth' get the jewelry?"

"Let's not jump to any conclusions," Dale said. "And let's be careful with the accusations."

"Fine," Tracy said. "What about the stores where Melissa Hogarth used her fraudulent credit cards? Has the security camera footage in any of those given you any more information?"

"Based on the footage we have, Arielle would not be incompatible with the person using the credit cards taken out in Melissa's name," Dale said.

"Right. So you'll investigate her?"

"I absolutely will," Dale said. "In fact, I think you might owe Cassie an apology."

Tracy had met Dale's wife many times. "Why is that?"

"She was looking forward to a nice, quiet evening in, and I'm about to ruin that plan. I'm headed right to the station to check this out."

"Please give Cassie my apologies," Tracy said. "And thank you."

Dale would find out whether it really was Arielle, and Tracy felt confident he would come to the same conclusion she had.

But now a new question surged in her mind. *Where is Arielle?*

Chapter Twenty-Four

Family dinner that night was a boisterous affair, as usual. Robin and her family, Jeff and Tracy's kids and grandkids, Amy and Miles and all their kids, Aunt Ruth and Uncle Marvin, and Tom and Angie were all in attendance. Tracy was glad she'd get to see her cousin one more time before he and his wife returned to Lincoln the following day.

Though the adults sat around Grandma Pearl's long dining table and the kids sat at a card table, they were still packed in tight. But Tracy wouldn't have it any other way. They talked, joked, and laughed, enjoying the meal and each other's company.

After everyone had helped themselves to seconds and thirds of fried chicken, Tom tapped his knife against his glass, and everyone fell silent. "Angie and I have had such a great time being here with you all this week and a half," he said.

Angie beamed at his side. They'd been in contact with the man who'd bought the watch from Malcolm, and he'd already agreed to return it, though Tracy was pretty sure Malcolm had had to refund his money. Still, they had been reassured that the watch would be on its way back to Tom soon, much to the family's relief.

"We've really loved feeling like a part of this community," Tom went on, "and being able to spend so much time around family. Thank you all for making us feel welcome."

"Why don't you move home?" Aunt Ruth said in her typical blunt fashion. "Then you could be here every week."

Several people around the table laughed, but Tom cleared his throat. "Actually, Mom, it's funny you should mention that."

Everyone froze, staring at Tom. "What?" Robin squawked.

"Angie and I were here this week for more than simply seeing you all, though that would have been worth it by itself. We were also here to do some shopping."

"*House* shopping," Angie clarified, winking at Tracy.

"You're kidding." Robin leaned forward, her hands on the table. "Are you really—?"

Tom smiled. "Yes, we really are. Lincoln has been good to us over the years, but we miss our families too much. We put in an offer on a house yesterday, and it was accepted today. We're moving home to Canton."

The table erupted in cheers and hoots, and Aunt Ruth sobbed happily.

"We're sorry we've been acting so strange," Angie said. "I know we've been a bit vague about where we were and what we were doing this past week, but we didn't want to say anything until we knew whether it was really going to happen or not."

"We toured a bunch of houses, and one really stood out," Tom said. "It's right in this neighborhood, so we'll be able to walk over for family dinners."

"Where? Which one?" Amy asked.

"The blue one that's for sale a few blocks over," Tom said.

"We'll be neighbors," Miles said, grinning.

"Hang on. Was one of the houses you visited out by the shopping center?" Tracy asked. The pieces started to fall into place in her mind. "Last Sunday?"

"It was," Tom said. "That's why we were over that way. I know you thought it was strange, and I'm sorry I couldn't tell you what we were really doing. Our hopes were already up, and we didn't want to risk raising yours and then disappointing all of you."

"I understand," Tracy said, though she wished they'd told her sooner. It explained so much—their caginess, what they were doing at the shopping center, their visit to town in general.

But it didn't explain everything. What about Angie's frequent trips to the bathroom during the progressive dinner, and the fact that she still barely touched anything on her plate, and how she appeared so wan and tired? If she wasn't reacting to guilt, what was she—

Wait a second.

Tracy studied her, and now that she was looking through the right lens, she could see what she had totally missed before. "Is there anything else you want to tell us?" she asked.

Angie laughed. "Again, we were waiting until we were sure."

Tracy clapped both hands over her mouth to keep from blurting the announcement before they could.

"We're having a baby," Tom said, a huge smile on his face. "Due in September. That's another reason we're moving home. We want our child to grow up like this, surrounded by family."

This time the shouts were even louder. Robin flew out of her chair and around the table to hug her brother, and Aunt Ruth's tears flowed afresh as she murmured, "God does answer prayer."

Tracy was thrilled for her cousin. Soon there would be another little face at family dinner. She wished Grandma Pearl were there, so she could see all the new members who had been added to her family in the past few years. She would have loved it. But Tracy felt that she did know, and that she was pleased. She couldn't imagine a more fitting tribute to their grandmother than gathering more members of the next generation around her table.

And now that Tom and Angie's strange behavior was explained, she could see how silly it had been to suspect them at all. Tom and Angie could never have stolen from any of them. They were family, like everyone else at the table. And soon they would be here every week.

Tracy couldn't wait.

Chapter Twenty-Five

Monday morning, Tracy woke early, filled with anxiety. As awesome as last night's news was, she couldn't stop thinking about Arielle and Millie, if Dale had investigated some more, and what he'd found out. It was too early to call him, and he wouldn't be able to tell her much anyway.

Well, Tracy knew how to get in touch with Millie. She hopped out of bed and went downstairs to make coffee. After a morning devotion, she made spinach and cheese omelets for breakfast.

When the food was gone and the dishes were done, Tracy sent a text to Robin.

Is Millie working today?

Robin texted back right away. Yes, starting at 1. I have to take Kai to the dentist this afternoon, so she's holding down the fort.

Great. Thanks. I'll plan to stop by the shop after 1 then. Everything okay?

Just have some questions for her, Tracy replied. It was mostly true.

It was a gray day, with occasional drizzling rain. April showers were supposed to bring May flowers, but they still bummed Tracy out. She dressed warmly, drank an extra cup of coffee, and then went to the office and got to work.

Annette had asked her to write a story about a high school senior in Lewistown who had started a program to connect volunteers with animal shelters. Tracy loved working on such heartwarming stories, especially if it meant a trip to a shelter to pet some sweet cats and dogs. She emailed the student to set up a time for an interview, and then she got lost in research for her next column until a voice behind her said, "Um, Tracy?"

Tracy turned around and smiled at Bethany. Since she'd discovered the young reporter's art, she hadn't paid much attention to her as a suspect—which meant she hadn't paid much attention to Bethany at all.

Bethany glanced around, as if to make sure no one was listening. Jake had left a few minutes before, so no one was within earshot.

"Hi." Tracy felt sheepish. "Hey, Robert West told me about your art. I checked it out, and I think it's beautiful."

"Thank you." She kept her voice low. "He told me he shared it with you, and I appreciate it. But the thing is, I don't really want a lot of people to know about it, so I wanted to ask if you would keep it quiet."

"Keep it quiet?" Tracy asked. "Why? It's beautiful. Don't you want to get the word out so you can sell more?"

"I really want to be a journalist," Bethany said. "Like, that's my dream. And I know that if certain people"—she nodded toward Eric's glass-walled office—"find out about the art, they'll think I'm not serious about this job."

"Why would anyone think that?" Tracy asked. "You're allowed to have hobbies and things you do outside of work. In fact, that's healthy. Work can't be your whole life."

Bethany frowned in confusion. "I always thought so too, but a few months ago I got up the courage to ask Eric about his career path, and he told me that to make it in journalism, it has to be your sole focus. He said he didn't go on a vacation or out with his friends or on dates for years when he was first starting out. Not until he'd established himself."

"That's awful." It also sounded entirely plausible, given Eric's personality. But that didn't mean it was what everyone had to do.

"He made it sound like that was what he expected of me too, if I was serious about this." Bethany grimaced. "And I am. But journalism doesn't pay all that well, and with my student loans and roommate issues, making a little extra on the side helps. Sometimes I get a good deal on a computer I know I can fix up a little and resell for more. Then I use the old parts in my art and make some money that way too. But I don't want Eric to know about it, or he'll think I'm not completely devoted to my career."

Tracy could see how important it was to Bethany. "Okay. I promise I'll keep it quiet."

"Thank you." Bethany let out a breath. "I really want this."

Tracy raised a finger. "But I want to also go on record to say that Eric's way is not the only path to a career in journalism. It is perfectly acceptable—advisable, even—to have a life outside of work. What matters is that you deliver articles on time and in good shape. You'll start to build up bylines, and that's what will help you move up in the ranks."

Bethany nodded. "I do hope to start writing more pieces soon, when Annette gives me the okay. And I hear you. But Eric's the boss, so I want to respect what he says."

Tracy understood Bethany's point. When the boss told her what was expected of her, it was hard for her to ignore it, even if she didn't agree with what he said.

"Well, your secret is safe with me," she said. "But for what it's worth, I think you should keep at it. It's so unique and beautiful."

"Thanks." Bethany smiled shyly. "I appreciate it." She returned to her desk.

Another mystery solved.

Tracy spent the rest of the morning working on her articles then ate the sandwich she'd brought for lunch.

Afterward, she hitched up her purse and walked to Pearls of Wisdom. She found Millie sorting through a stack of old postcards.

At the sight of her, Millie's face twisted in—what? Dread? Fear? Tracy couldn't tell.

"Hi, Millie."

"I already spoke with Sergeant Leewright," Millie said sharply. "And I told him that Arielle had nothing to do with it, so he's barking up the wrong tree."

Millie was in denial, and understandably so. Tracy was sure she'd feel similarly if someone accused Amy. But she needed to figure out a way to break through that. Tracy had a feeling Dale had already hit her with the facts—that they knew Arielle had sold Tracy's laptop, that they were pretty sure she was the real person behind the fake Melissa Hogarth, and that her disappearance heightened their suspicions. If telling Millie the cold hard facts hadn't convinced her, Tracy was pretty sure repeating them would make Millie double down. She'd seen it happen many times, and she suspected that she would have to use another strategy if she wanted to persuade Millie to help her find Arielle.

"I honestly just want to talk to her, Millie," Tracy said. "I'm sure there's an explanation for all of this. If I could talk to her, it would all become clear. Could you ask her to meet with me? I'm not a police officer, so she has no reason to be afraid of me. I could meet her wherever she's comfortable. Maybe at your place or Café Chew?"

Tracy knew Arielle wasn't in Canton. There was no way she could be. But she had to get Millie to admit as much.

"I don't know." Millie's bottom lip trembled. "I'm not sure that's possible."

Tracy peered into her face but kept her voice kind and understanding. "Where is she, Millie?"

Millie's face crumpled, and she burst into tears. "I don't know where she went. And the truth is, I haven't seen her in more than a week. When I woke up last Sunday, she was gone."

"Oh, Millie," Tracy said with a combination of compassion and frustration. If Millie had admitted that a week ago, they could have saved so much time and effort, not to mention police hours. Why hadn't she said that Arielle had fled after the party from day one?

But Tracy knew the answer deep in her bones. Arielle was family. Millie couldn't comprehend that someone she loved would have done something so hurtful, so she'd refused to believe it, even when the truth stared her right in the face. People were good at seeing what they expected to and refusing to perceive anything beyond that. Tracy had done the same thing with Tom and Angie, missing the obvious signs that Angie was pregnant, because she was focused on nefarious reasons for her strange behavior. Not that it was easy to believe anything awful of a loved one, as Simon Dimas was learning firsthand.

"Do you know where she went?" Tracy asked.

Millie shook her head. "I thought she went home to St. Louis, but when I called her roommate, Maya said that Arielle hadn't paid rent in three months and she'd kicked her out." Millie sniffled. "That must have been why she decided to come for a visit. Not because she wanted to see us, but because she was homeless and needed a place to crash."

"I'm so sorry."

Millie pressed her lips together then said, "My parents are frantic with worry."

Tracy dug a pack of tissues out of her purse and offered it to the distraught woman. Millie took it with a quiet thank-you, pulled out a tissue, and dabbed her eyes.

"I should have known. We were so glad to see her that we didn't question it, but it was strange. I can see that now. She hasn't come to visit for a few years, so showing up out of the blue like she did—well, we should have known."

"You love your sister, Millie. Of course you were glad to see her. And why would you suspect that she'd been kicked out?" Tracy asked. "No one would guess that."

Millie wrung her hands. "I guess it wasn't that out of character, if I'm honest. It's not that I couldn't have figured it out. It was more that I didn't want to see it, I guess."

Tracy thought of several different responses, but she decided to hold her tongue and see what Millie would say next.

"I've told you about my brother." Millie plucked a new tissue from the pack. "He's gotten some help from a rehab program and is just now getting back on his feet. Mom and Dad and I have been so excited about that." She wiped her eyes. "But Arielle...that's a different story."

Millie blew out a breath. "It hasn't been easy to watch her make one bad decision after another, pursuing her pie in the sky." She fell silent, staring contemplatively at the pack of tissues.

"Can you think of anywhere she might have gone?" Tracy asked. "It would be so helpful to be able to talk to her."

"I can't," Millie said. "This time I think she's really gotten herself in a pickle, and I can't help her, because I honestly don't know where she's gone."

"Does she have any friends she might have moved in with?" Tracy suggested. "Any places she might have gone to hide?"

"Not a clue," Millie replied. "Her life is so far removed from mine these days that I never know what she's up to. She doesn't tell me things anymore. She could be halfway to California for all I know."

Her tone was so different from when the conversation started. The brittle edge in her voice had given way to a softer, sadder sound. One that was more realistic about the possibilities.

"We have reason to think she might have been in La Grange earlier this week," Tracy said. "Do you have any idea what connection she might have there?"

"She's still in the area, then?" Millie sounded hopeful.

"It seems she was at that point," Tracy said.

"Let's hope she's still around," Millie said. "But I don't know where she would be."

"We'll do our best to find her," Tracy said.

Millie handed the rest of the tissue pack to her, ducking her head. "Let's hope she's okay."

⋆ Chapter Twenty-Six ⋆

Tracy was making coffee Tuesday morning when Anna called her.

"Is everything okay?" Tracy asked. Anna didn't usually call so early. "What's wrong?" Was it something with one of the kids? With Chad?

"I'm so sorry. I didn't wake you up, did I?"

"No, I was up." Jeff woke her when he went out for a run, and she'd lazed around for a while, trying to go back to sleep, before giving up and crawling out of bed. "Are the kids okay?"

"Everyone is fine," Anna assured her. "But I was up scrolling through social media last night while I was feeding Elizabeth, and I saw the strangest thing. The app I was using suggests new content creators you might want to follow. Sometimes it's right, while others are way out of left field. Anyway, last night it suggested a new channel from a beauty influencer, and I thought, why not? I usually stick to ones in the home design category to check out the competition, but what else am I going to do at three a.m.?"

Anna wasn't usually this chatty, so Tracy resisted the urge to hurry her along and instead let her talk.

"Anyway, I watched some of her videos, and I recognized something about her, but I couldn't put my finger on what. I watched a video about how to use a flat iron to make waves, then one about creating a smoky eye. I was thinking there was no way the channel would take off, because there was nothing new there, but I kept watching because I was trying to figure out how I knew her."

"And did you?"

"I sure did," Anna said. "After a few more videos, I worked it out. This girl had blond hair, not dark hair, but other than that it was so obvious I felt kind of silly for not recognizing it sooner."

"Who was it?" Tracy already suspected the answer, but she wanted to hear Anna say it.

"It was Arielle."

"Millie's sister?"

"Yeah. The one who was at the progressive dinner. And in one video, she's in front of a mirror, and I caught a glimpse of a ring light. Now I'm not saying she couldn't have her own. After all, it's not like I own the only ring light ever made. However, her channel is brand new, and all of her videos have been posted in the past week. Which makes me think that's around when she actually got the light, and that timing was very interesting to me."

Arielle—who had previously tried to make it as a travel writer, a salesperson, and who knew what else—had apparently turned her attention to a new venture.

"Can you send me a link?" Tracy asked.

"Sending it right now." A moment later, Tracy heard a beep as a text from Anna arrived.

"I'll check it out," Tracy said.

"I'd appreciate that. Let me know if I'm totally off base here," Anna said. "I don't want to go around slinging false accusations."

"I'm sure you're right, actually, but like I said, I'll see for myself."

"Thanks,"

"Thank you for bringing it to my attention. I'll get back to you soon."

They hung up, and after she'd poured herself a cup of coffee, Tracy tapped on the link and found herself on a page with half a dozen videos from an "Aria French." BEAUTY INFLUENCER, GLAMOR GIRL, according to the bio.

Tracy had no doubt it was Arielle, regardless of the blond hair. She had dyed her hair or donned a wig, like the picture on the Melissa Hogarth ID, but it was unmistakably her. Tracy scrolled through her videos, and they were as Anna had said. Tracy didn't usually watch beauty-influencer content, so she had no idea how Arielle's compared to others, but she didn't see anything special about the channel. She had heard of others getting paid to teach the masses about modern beauty trends and how to achieve them, but from what she understood, there had to be something unique about the creator or their content for the person to be able to make a living at it. She didn't see that happening based on what Arielle had posted.

And at that moment, Tracy didn't really care. She was much more interested in finding her. She sent the link to Dale Leewright, explaining that Anna had found the videos and they were sure it was Arielle. Then she sat back, sipping her coffee. There had to be a way to figure out where the videos had been filmed. Perhaps she could piece it together from the details she could pick up.

She went through the videos again, ignoring what Arielle was doing in each one and concentrating more on the background. In a hair-curling video, Arielle sat at a wooden table in front of big sliding glass doors framed by wooden wall panels. Trees heavy with buds filled the outdoors behind her.

In the video about making a smoky eye, she was in a bathroom with pink tiles. In a video about making a salt scrub, she was in a kitchen with butcher-block counters and an avocado-green tile backsplash.

Tracy found it all very strange. She hadn't watched many influencer videos in her life, but weren't they usually set in some dreamy location the audience would want to visit, or show some luxury they would want to aspire to? Anna's videos were like that, typically created in her gorgeous kitchen. The very few influencer videos Tracy had seen were visually appealing. But Arielle's videos were set in a house that appeared to be stuck in the 1970s.

Maybe Millie would know where this particular house was. Tracy sent her an email including screenshots of the video, in case she recognized anything. Tracy hoped that if they could figure out where the videos were filmed, they could find Arielle.

Sadie laid her head in Tracy's lap, and Tracy stroked the dog's ears as she tried to make sense of the situation. She didn't want to wait around and see if Millie recognized the location. There was no telling when Millie would even check her email. How could Tracy figure out where the videos were filmed before then?

She took another sip of coffee, and then the answer was so obvious she wanted to smack herself in the forehead.

She picked up her phone again and called Anna back. "Hi, it's me again," she said. "That's totally her. Good find."

"I knew it," Anna replied.

"Is there a way to figure out where a video was filmed?" Tracy asked. "Any kind of geolocation on the data or anything like that?"

Anna paused. "You know, there should be. The app tracks a lot of details, things like location and what kinds of content you interact with. A lot of people think it shouldn't be allowed to do that, because they worry about who has access to that information. And to be fair, it is kind of alarming if you don't know where it's going. The point is, I'm sure the information exists somewhere. I just don't know who would know how to figure that kind of thing out. In fact, that's probably why this video came up for me, to be honest. The algorithm tends to serve up content created in your general area. It knows where I am when I'm scrolling, and it knows where people are when they post their videos."

"But to figure it out, you'd need someone who was really into computers and programming, right?" Tracy asked. Something had begun to percolate in her mind.

"Exactly," said Anna. "A hacker would be ideal, but I don't know anyone like that."

Tract felt a smile curve her lips. "Don't worry about it. I think I do."

Chapter Twenty-Seven

It was a school day. Tracy didn't want to wait until after three, so her best shot was to get to Caleb before he left for school. She left her coffee mug on the counter, ran upstairs and put on jeans and a sweater, shoved her feet into shoes, and pulled on a coat.

Sadie whined as Tracy raced toward the door. "Jeff will take you out when he gets home after his run," Tracy promised over her shoulder.

She hopped in the car, patted her pocket to make sure she had her phone, and then took off. School buses already trundled through the streets. Did Caleb take a bus to school? Would he still be home? Tracy braked as a school bus put on its flashing lights and stuck out its stop sign. As she waited for the bus to start again, she had a moment of recognition at how impulsively she was acting, rushing across town, hoping to catch a teenage boy before he left for school so he could help her hack a video.

Well, she might be impulsive, but she wanted answers too much to turn back. As soon as the bus started moving again, Tracy hit the gas and made her way to the section of town where Sharon and Caleb lived. She parked behind the car in their driveway then hurried to the door and rang the bell.

Sharon opened the door. "Oh. Hi, Tracy." She sounded wary. Her hair was gathered in a messy bun, and she wore yoga pants and a sweatshirt that said MIAMI BEACH, FL.

"I'm sorry to bother you so early," Tracy said. "I think I know who took the laptops and the phone, and I was wondering if Caleb might be able to help me figure out where the person is. I was hoping he could use his programming skills to help me."

"He's about to leave for school," Sharon said. "I don't think—"

"I can help," Caleb said, appearing beside his mother. He wore baggy jeans and a sweater, his black backpack over one shoulder. Given the opportunity to work with computers, he was more animated than she'd ever seen him. "What do you need?"

"It's a video that was posted on an app. My daughter-in-law Anna said there might be a way to find information on it that would tell us where it was taken," Tracy said. "But she doesn't know how to do it."

"You bet," Caleb said. "That's not hard. Where's the video?"

"It's on my phone," Tracy said. "It can wait until after school—"

Caleb interrupted her. "I have study hall first period, so I can go to school late. If you send me the video, I'll work on it before I head in."

"That's okay?" Tracy asked.

"Sure." Caleb shrugged. "It'll be more interesting than the other stuff I could be doing."

"You still have to do your trigonometry," Sharon said, her voice stern.

"I will, Mom. This shouldn't take very long, so I can finish trig afterward. It's important. I want to help. Please?"

Sharon appraised him then smiled. "All right."

"Thanks, Mom." He looked back at Tracy. "Can you send me a link?"

"I'll text it to you," Tracy said. "What's your number?"

He gave her his cell number, and Tracy sent the video. A moment later, he held up his phone and said, "Got it. I'll let you know what I find."

As he disappeared, likely to his room, Tracy thought it was the happiest she'd ever seen him. She supposed that made sense. Like anyone else, he needed to be needed. Plus, she'd given him an excuse to do something he loved.

"Thank you," Tracy said to Sharon.

Sharon gave her a wry smile. "I figured it must be important to pull you out of the house this early."

Tracy laughed. "It is. I'm really hoping this is the proof we need to find the thief once and for all. We're pretty sure we finally know who it is."

"I'm glad to hear it," Sharon said. Tracy knew she meant it for several reasons, not the least of which was that it would clear Caleb's name once and for all. "I'm sure Caleb will let you know when he has it. He's extremely responsive when it comes to computers, as I'm sure you've noticed. Thank you for giving him this opportunity. Perhaps it'll open his mind to the possibility of using his skills as a career."

"That would be great. I definitely saw how he lit up when I asked him to help me. He'll find his way, Sharon. Thank you again." Tracy returned to her car and drove home.

A freshly showered Jeff was drinking coffee and reading his Bible when she walked in. "Where'd you go?"

"To talk to Caleb Presley before he left for school." Tracy went to pour herself another cup of coffee while she explained about her calls with Anna that morning.

"Can I see the account you found?" Jeff asked. Tracy pulled up the channel and handed him her phone, and he watched a few of the videos in silence.

"It's her," Tracy said. "Arielle."

"I can see that," Jeff said. "Now don't interrupt. I'm learning all about how to create beachy waves in my hair using nothing but my regular old flat iron."

Tracy laughed and took the phone back. "Anna thinks there's a geolocation thing on the app. She says if we can find it, it might show us where the videos were filmed."

"So you went to ask Caleb to help you figure it out," Jeff said. "I see. Good thing you have a hacker in your back pocket."

"His mom appreciated my giving him a positive outlet for his passion." She paused for a moment. "Besides, what he's doing is actually important to the case. If he can get the location where the videos were posted and Arielle is still there, we'll be able to wrap this whole thing up."

"We?" Jeff echoed. "Don't you mean the police?"

Tracy flapped a hand at him. "Semantics. Whose side are you on, anyway?"

Jeff chuckled. "Did you try asking Millie to see if she recognized the location before you engaged a hacker?"

"Yes, I did try the simplest solution first. I haven't heard from her yet." She checked her phone to see if she'd missed a message from Millie, Dale, or Caleb, even though Caleb had probably barely had time to get started on the video.

"I'm sure she'll get back to you when she sees it," Jeff said.

"Probably, but you know how bad I am at sitting around twiddling my thumbs."

"That's true. But don't you need to go to the newspaper today?"

Tracy sighed. "I suppose, but it's not nearly as exciting as this is."

The sound of Jeff's laughter followed her upstairs.

When she was ready for the day, Tracy checked her phone again on her way to the car, but there were no messages, much to her disappointment. She drove to work and tried to focus on writing her article about the program to connect volunteers with animal shelters. She'd gone to Lewistown and interviewed the high school senior behind it yesterday afternoon, so this morning was about typing up the story. If she could focus on it.

She had barely gotten started when a phone call from Dale broke her concentration. "I've got to hand it to you, Tracy. I don't know how you keep finding these clues."

"To be fair, Anna found this one," Tracy said.

"Either way, I've sent it to our IT team to find out what they can tell me about it," Dale said. "Hopefully this is the clue we need to find her."

Tracy decided not to mention that she'd put her own version of an IT team on it as well. He would tell her to stay out of it again, and he probably wouldn't be thrilled with the prospect of a teenage hacker digging into his investigation.

"I sent Millie some stills to see if she recognized the location," Tracy said. "But I haven't heard from her yet."

There was a brief silence as Dale likely swallowed a lecture about her moving without his permission. Finally, he said, "I'll check in with her as well. Thanks, Tracy."

Tracy went back to working on her story. She'd roughed out the first paragraph when her phone buzzed again, this time with a text from Caleb.

Tracy opened the text and saw an image of a map with a blue dot marking a location. The map showed a rural area in the southeastern part of the county, between Durham and La Grange. The dot was along a road that mirrored a small river as it wound through the county. 28437 ROUTE 587, it said under the dot.

Tracy texted back. THAT'S WHERE THE VIDEOS WERE FILMED?

THAT'S WHAT THE GEOLOCATION DATA SAYS, he replied. NO IDEA WHAT'S THERE, BUT THAT'S WHERE I'D START LOOKING FOR HER.

GREAT WORK, CALEB. THANK YOU.

She grabbed her purse and dashed through the office and out to her car. She programmed the address Caleb had given her into her phone's GPS. Twenty-five minutes. That's where Arielle had been this whole time? Less than half an hour away?

Tracy called Millie. It would be better to have her along, but the phone rang through to voice mail. Tracy tried her again, with the same result, and then she sent a text. No response.

Well, there was no time to lose. Tracy made one more call before she started off, heading out of town and into the farmland that surrounded Canton. Halfway through the drive, the adrenaline started to wear off, and Tracy realized what she was about to do and how potentially dangerous it was. She didn't know what she'd find when she got there, if anything. Arielle might not be there. Or she might be there, but she might not be alone, or she might be uninterested in coming quietly. She could be surrounded by a cache of guns—that far out in the country, it wasn't at all unusual. Was Tracy being irresponsible, going out to confront Arielle on her own?

Maybe. Probably. All she knew for sure was that she couldn't go back. She was going to get answers once and for all.

Chapter Twenty-Eight

The little cabin stood in a stand of woods along the Fabius River, set well back from the road. It was a sweet A-frame, with a wide wooden porch and a cleared parking area in front of the house. Two cars were parked there when Tracy pulled up—an older, beat-up Toyota, and a newer blue Ford. One she recognized right away. It belonged to Millie Ettlinger.

What was Millie doing here? Tracy supposed she would find out when she got inside. She took a deep breath and walked up the wooden steps. She knocked on the door. There was no sound from within. Tracy waited, and then she knocked again. Again, nothing but silence.

Tracy tentatively laid her hand on the doorknob. She wouldn't go in. She'd open the door and call out to the sisters. Perhaps they hadn't heard her knocking. Or something terrible had happened inside when Millie had come to confront her sister. What if she was—

She halted that thought before she could finish it. She was being alarmist. She twisted the knob and found it unlocked. She pushed the door open and called "Millie?"

She was looking into an open living room and kitchen area. Tracy recognized the walls and the big sliding glass doors at the rear of the house from the video. She recognized the avocado-green tile from the video as well.

And she recognized Jeff's laptop on the kitchen table and Anna's ring light set up in front of it. There was Anna's phone too.

"Millie?" Tracy called again.

She stepped inside and spotted Millie and Arielle standing near a stairway on the left that led from the ground floor to a loft that overlooked the open main floor.

"Don't take another step." Arielle brandished a fireplace poker. "Just go, and we can pretend this never happened."

"Give me that." Millie snatched at the poker, but Arielle dodged and held it out of her reach.

"I mean it," Arielle said. "No one has to get hurt."

"No one has to get hurt anyway, Arielle," Millie said. "Put it down. This isn't how you want this to go."

"No, what I want is not to go to jail," Arielle said.

Tracy noticed that Arielle's hands trembled, making the poker shiver in midair. She might be desperate, but she certainly didn't seem to be a hardened criminal. But that didn't make her any less dangerous.

"You have to promise you won't tell anyone where I am," Arielle insisted. "Say you won't tell the police, then get out of here."

"What are you doing, Arielle?" Millie was pleading with her now. "Please put the poker down."

"When did you get here, Millie?" Tracy asked. "Did you know where she was all along?"

"I didn't." Millie shook her head. "I had no idea, Tracy. You have to believe me. Even when you mentioned she'd been in La Grange, it never occurred to me that she might have holed up in Grandpa's old hunting cabin. It's not in La Grange proper, but that's the closest real town. It wasn't until you sent me those videos this morning that I recognized the background and realized she must have been here."

"But you didn't tell Dale?" Tracy asked.

Millie shook her head. "No. Why would I tell him when I didn't know for sure she was still here?"

"Arielle, please put the poker down," Tracy said, her tone much more stern than Millie's had been. "Don't do this to Millie. Not after everything she's done for you. Think of your sister the way she always thinks of you."

"I'll put it down when you promise not to tell anyone what you saw or where I am," Arielle said.

Tracy wasn't about to make a promise she had no intention of keeping. But she also didn't want Arielle to hurt Millie. She could duck right back out the door, but then what would keep Arielle from escaping or, worse, attacking her own sister?

She had no choice. No matter how dangerous it was, she would have to stall while she tried to figure out her next step, and she would have to risk Arielle losing her temper and attacking one of them with the poker.

"Your plan was to become a beauty influencer?" Tracy asked. "After travel writing didn't pan out?"

"Travel writing is a harder gig than you'd think," Arielle said. "I thought I would get to take lots of glamorous vacations, but all it got me was a bunch of layovers in Cleveland and a pile of debt."

"And you needed my husband's laptop to make your beauty influencing dreams come true?"

"I needed capital," Arielle corrected her. "I sold the jewelry right away. Your laptop was easy enough to unload, but I kept the better one for myself. And that light is just what I needed. I saved myself a couple hundred dollars when I took that."

"And the credits cards? All the ones you opened in a fake name?"

She shrugged. "They can't prove that was me."

Actually, Dale was working on a way to do exactly that, but Tracy wasn't about to say that out loud, not while Arielle still had the poker in her hand.

"Did you really think you would get away with it?" Tracy was running out of ways to distract Arielle, and she hoped the young woman couldn't sense her rising anxiety about it. "Surely you had to know that the police would find out eventually."

"Oh yeah?" Arielle laughed. "Where are the police now? All I see is you, and you're going to walk away like this never happened."

She'd barely gotten the words out when they all heard the sound of wheels crunching over the gravel of the driveway.

Panic flooded Arielle's face. "Who did you tell?"

"It's time to put the poker down, Arielle," Tracy said. "That's Officer Leewright out there."

"You told the cops?" Arielle shrieked.

"Arielle, stop. It's over." Millie struggled to get the poker from her sister.

Footsteps pounded up the steps, and then Dale burst into the cabin. "Police!"

With a scream, Arielle wrenched the poker away from Millie and hurled it.

Chapter Twenty-Nine

It took Tracy a moment to register that the poker had hit the doorframe right next to where Dale stood. She breathed a sigh of relief that Arielle had missed as the heavy metal rod fell to the floor with a clang, leaving no more harm than a deep gouge in the wooden doorframe.

"It's time to stop this, Arielle." Nothing on Dale's face betrayed fear in spite of the close call.

Arielle didn't move. She stood as if rooted to the spot, shaking uncontrollably.

"Come on, Arielle." Millie's voice trembled, whether from fear or relief or anger, Tracy couldn't say. She'd just watched her sister try to take down a police officer. The poker could have killed Dale, or at least done serious damage. "It's time to give up. We have to go talk to Sergeant Leewright."

"I won't go to prison," Arielle said.

"I'm sure we'll be able to work something out," Millie said soothingly. "Let's go talk to Dale. He's a good lawman. He'll listen and be fair."

Slowly, almost as if she weren't in her own body, Arielle let Millie lead her to stand in front of Dale.

Dale put Arielle's hands behind her back and clicked handcuffs around her wrists.

"Don't worry," Millie continued. "Mom and Dad and I will help. We'll get a good lawyer. We'll do everything we can."

It broke Tracy's heart to see how much Millie loved her sister, even now. Even when her guilt was undeniable and she'd tried to do something horrible. Even then, Millie loved her sister and wanted to help her.

But that was what love was like. It never gave up on someone, even when they did the wrong thing. It always saw the best in people, even when their actions didn't support it. Love drove Millie to defend her sister, though she knew Arielle was wrong.

Tracy was glad Arielle had someone in her corner who loved her that way. What she'd done was wrong in so many ways, and Tracy had yet to see her show an iota of remorse for it. But the fact that she had someone who loved her, who would work to get her the fairest treatment, made Tracy think things might work out for her after all.

As she watched Arielle being led to the police car, Tracy was grateful that nothing worse had happened. She thanked God for giving her the foresight to call Dale on her way to the cabin, that the poker had missed, and that everyone had walked out of there under their own power. She thanked God that this nightmare would soon be over, and they'd soon get their stolen items returned to them. That things would go back to normal. That soon, she would open her home up to strangers again, trusting that even though bad things sometimes happened, most people were good.

Dale climbed into the front seat of the police car, and Tracy pulled Millie in for a hug.

Millie's strength deserted her, and she buried her face in Tracy's shoulder, sobbing, "I'm so sorry. I'm so, so sorry."

As Tracy watched Dale back out of the driveway, she thought about the love Millie had for Arielle and was grateful she had so much love in her own life.

"Come on," Tracy said after a moment. "Let's go. Maybe they'll let you see her at the station."

Millie sniffed. "Thanks, Tracy."

"It's all going to be all right," Tracy murmured.

As she walked Millie to her car, she realized she meant it. They were both surrounded by the kind of love that never lets go.

The kind that forgives.

That believes in its loved ones, no matter what.

And that was more than enough.

Dear Reader,

Many years ago, my husband and I came home to our third-floor Brooklyn apartment after a night out, and it took us a minute to figure out something was off. After a few minutes, one of us asked, "Where's my computer?" A minute of frantic searching later—it was a small apartment, so it didn't take that long—we found that both of our laptops were gone, as were our iPods (I told you it was a long time ago). We also discovered that the window that led to the fire escape wasn't closed correctly, and suddenly, we understood. Someone had climbed the fire escape, found our window unlocked, and helped themselves to our electronics.

We called the police, and they were very nice and dusted our place for fingerprints. But we felt dumb (how could we have left the window unlocked?) as well as violated (someone had been in our space!) and angry (how could someone take our things?). I also felt stupidly upset that the thief hadn't understood that the art on our walls was way more valuable than the electronics, but I guess large paintings by emerging artists aren't as easy to unload on the streets of Brooklyn as a laptop.

In the days after the theft, I visited the pawn shops in the area to try to find our things, with no luck. I did not enjoy the experience, as you might have gathered from the way Tracy responds to them in this book.

A few days after the theft, my husband was using a real version of the Locate app to try to track his computer when it appeared online. He called the police immediately and told them where it was. We were so excited! But the police basically shrugged. They weren't going to chase down the laptop like we thought. It wasn't a great neighborhood, and there were more important things for them to do than worry about a couple of yuppies whose MacBooks would be replaced by insurance anyway. They didn't come out and say it in so many words, but that was the gist of their response. In the grand scheme of things, it wasn't really that big of a deal, even though it felt like it to us at the time. Our insurance replaced our electronics, and we eventually moved on from that apartment and into a better neighborhood in Brooklyn.

Although I wish that experience had never happened, I was able to draw on it for this book, and I guess that's a good thing. I suppose it's true that everything can be fodder for novels. I hope I was able to channel Tracy's sense of violation, outrage, and hurt when she discovered what happened. And I hope you enjoyed reading this as much as I enjoyed writing it.

Best,
Beth Adams

About The Author

Beth Adams lives in Brooklyn, New York, with her husband and two young daughters. When she's not writing, she spends her time cleaning up after two devious cats and trying to find time to read mysteries.

COLLECTIBLES from GRANDMA'S ATTIC

Antique Watches

A few years ago, I met a guy who collected antique watches. I remember thinking how odd a hobby that seemed to be. In a world of watches that can text and make phone calls and play music and track my workouts and call 911 for me if I'm in a car accident, why would I want a watch that just tells time?

But I love antiques, so I decided to unravel the appeal. When I started researching, I began to understand that watches, like any other piece of the past, have a rich and fascinating history. I learned how the first watches were miniature spring-loaded clocks and that a German man named Peter Henlein, a locksmith in Nuremburg, Germany, is credited with inventing the first one in the sixteenth century. These early portable clocks were typically worn around the neck as a pendant, but in the seventeenth century, men began keeping their watches in their pockets. The first wristwatch is credited to Abraham-Louis Breguet, and it was designed for the queen of Naples in 1810. At first, wristwatches were usually worn by women, but the need for synchronized movement of the military led to the growth of wristwatches for men.

As technology improved—in winding mechanisms, in case materials, and in production—and mass production became possible, watches became ubiquitous, and many of the famous watch brands we now recognize began to emerge.

For the collector, there are many interesting and iconic watch models that mark major steps forward in watchmaking. Some such technological advances seem quaint now—the addition of a second hand, for instance, or a calendar date on the watch face. But others, like waterproofing and the ability to keep accurate time deep in the ocean or in outer space, are truly impressive feats of engineering.

It turns out that antique watches, like any other piece of the past, offer a fascinating glimpse into history.

SOMETHING DELICIOUS *from* GRANDMA PEARL'S RECIPE BOX

Spring Pea Tart

This recipe uses store-bought frozen puff pastry, but feel free to make your own if you prefer (and have lots of extra time in your day!). If you've never worked with puff pastry before, it can seem scary at first, but trust me, it's magic. The layers of pastry and butter that rise in the oven make such a delicious base for this fresh and light taste of spring.

Ingredients:

- 1 sheet frozen puff pastry, thawed and trimmed to a square
- 1½ cups frozen peas
- 1 cup whole-milk ricotta
- 3 tablespoons finely chopped fresh mint, divided, plus small whole leaves for garnish
- 2 teaspoons minced lemon zest
- Salt and freshly ground pepper, to taste
- ¼ cup parsley
- 2 green onions, sliced thin
- Fresh lemon juice, to taste

Directions:

Preheat oven to 400 degrees and line baking sheet with parchment paper. Place thawed puff pastry on parchment paper and bake for 10 to 12 minutes, or until puffed. Remove from oven, top with another sheet of parchment paper and another baking sheet, and return to oven. Continue baking another 10 to 12 minutes, until crispy and golden. Remove from oven and set aside to cool.

Bring a pot of salted water to boil, and boil peas just until they float to the surface—don't overcook or they'll be mushy. Drain and rinse under cold water. Reserve ⅓ cup peas. Combine remaining peas, ricotta, and 1 tablespoon mint in a food processor. Stir in lemon zest, salt, and pepper.

In a small bowl, combine parsley, remaining mint, green onions, and reserved peas. Add salt and lemon juice, to taste. Spread ricotta mixture over cooled pastry then top with parsley-and-green onion mixture. Garnish with whole mint cut into pieces, and serve.

Read on for a sneak peek of another exciting book in the Secrets from Grandma's Attic series!

Coming Home
By DeAnna Julie Dodson

"You wouldn't dare!" Amy Allen-Anderson snatched at the photograph her laughing sister, Tracy Doyle, held out of her reach. "That's the worst of all my school pictures."

"It's not so bad," Tracy said, handing it over at last. "Miles would love to see it, and so would your kids."

Amy and Tracy had a long history of bringing their families together on a Sunday to share a meal and time together. That afternoon, Amy had sent her husband and four children back home after lunch so their kids wouldn't know what she was up to. Tracy's history-professor husband, Jeff, was in his home office, grading papers. That gave Amy and Tracy a chance to go up into the attic and dig through photos.

"We haven't even been married for six months, and you're already trying to scare him off," Amy said.

"Don't be such a drama queen. You were twelve when this picture was taken. Everybody goes through an awkward stage."

"I look like I stuck my finger in a light socket."

Tracy snickered. "Mom told you not to perm your own hair."

"I know." Amy groaned. "But she did hers, so I figured I could do mine too. I was wrong." She shook her head. "So, so wrong."

"And just in time for school pictures," Tracy said.

"Sadly, that was the point. It was a hard-earned lesson."

Amy blotted a touch of sweat from her upper lip. The mid-May temperature was climbing toward eighty in Canton, and the attic in Tracy's house, once their Grandma Pearl's, wasn't air-conditioned. "Maybe we ought to haul a couple of these boxes downstairs where it's cooler."

"Good idea." Tracy handed her another photo from the box. "I'll trade my eleventh-grade shoulder pads for your seventh-grade hair."

"You were very stylish at the time." Amy chuckled. "Though maybe there are some things that should never again see the light of day."

"You're the one who thought the kids would like to see our old school pictures."

"The cute ones, Tracy. The cute ones."

"They're all cute," Tracy assured her. "We were young. Look at this one."

She pulled out Amy's first-grade picture. She wore a pink dress and a matching bow in her hair, which had been curled for the occasion. Her platinum-blond locks had certainly darkened over the years.

"You were so tiny back then," Tracy said. "Such a precious little dumpling."

Amy made a pained face. "Can we avoid terms like that?"

"I think you should definitely show Miles this one," Tracy insisted. "He'll fall in love with you all over again."

"Fine, but please don't ever call me a dumpling in front of him. I'll never hear the end of it."

"Okay. I'll behave. Let's get cool again."

They each grabbed a couple of boxes marked Photos, carried them down to Tracy's comfortable living room, and settled themselves on the couch.

Amy spread a handful of photos on the coffee table and started sorting through them. "We don't need to spend all day on this. A few school pictures will do."

Tracy sifted through the same box. "How about this one? I still think that's one of the best you ever took."

The photo was a smaller version of Amy's high-school graduation portrait. Her hair was permed in this one too, but it had been professionally done, giving her honey-blond locks soft curls instead of frizzy ones.

"Yeah," Amy said wistfully. "Mom and Dad liked that one too."

"It hung in their living room until they passed." Tracy opened another box. "They never threw away a single photo of either of us."

"I'm glad." Amy pulled out more pictures. "This one is sweet."

She showed Tracy a photo of themselves when they were little girls, Amy maybe four years old and Tracy about eight. They were sitting on Grandma Pearl's front porch with their cousins, Robin and Tom.

"Aw, how precious," Tracy said. "Tom really was a little dumpling back then. I remember how much he waddled when he was learning to walk."

"So cute," Amy said. "By the way, have you heard any updates about him and Angie moving here? I know they'd like to be settled before she has the baby, but I haven't heard a date yet."

"Nothing new. They're negotiating closing costs from what I've been hearing, and they need to change one room into a nursery. Fortunately, that can be done after the move."

"I'm sure they'll get it worked out, and we'll support them however we can."

They went through pictures, stopping to comment on various ones, until Tracy started laughing again.

"What now?" Amy demanded.

"You on your first birthday." Tracy handed over the photo. "You have your whole face and both hands in the cake."

"Good thing Mom thought to make me my own little cake and keep the big one for those who could use forks. And I seem to remember…" Amy dug around for something she'd caught a glimpse of earlier. "Aha! You weren't much better."

She brought out a picture of Tracy at her own first birthday party, with chocolate ice cream all over her hands and face.

"You're only one once, right?" Tracy said with a grin. "I think I'll put this on the refrigerator."

Amy chuckled as she went back to sorting through photos, and then she stopped again. "Speaking of birthdays, Miles has one coming up on the thirtieth of the month, and I'm really stuck about what to get him."

"I thought there might be another reason why you wanted him to take the kids home and leave you here for a while." Tracy pulled out another handful of pictures to sort.

"The problem is that he's used to buying whatever he wants. I want to do something for him that he hasn't thought of, something he'd never do for himself."

"So something beyond your typical ties and golf balls kind of thing."

"Exactly. I'd like to get rid of that dilapidated old shed in the backyard, but I guess that would be a present for me rather than him."

"I don't blame you. Does he actually use it?"

Amy wrinkled her nose. "He never even goes inside. The roof leaks, so he cleared it out and cluttered the garage with all the stuff. I wish he'd have it torn down already. Then we could either have more space in the yard or put up something nice in its place."

"I think it would be tough to pull that off as a birthday surprise. Has he mentioned anything he'd like someday? Something he thinks would be too much of a hassle now? Or maybe something he's put off since you and the kids moved in. How's that going, with six of you in the house now?"

Amy grinned at her sister. "We are kind of a mini Brady Bunch, aren't we? But you know, especially since the girls wanted to share a room, we still have plenty of space." She snapped her fingers. "I've got it. Back when we first started seeing each other again, Miles mentioned wanting a space of his own."

"A man cave!" Tracy crowed. "That's a great idea."

"We could use the room that was originally going to be Jana's for it." Amy was surprised she hadn't thought of it before. "I'd love to do that, but do you think there'd be time?"

"How much do you want to do?"

"I don't think it would take much. He loves all the local teams, but especially the St. Louis Blues, so I could use their blue and gold in the room. I'd put in a nice recliner or maybe a recliner couch, a big screen TV mounted on the wall, and a good surround-sound system. Miles has a lot of books, but he also has some sports memorabilia, some autographed pucks and sticks, a couple of baseballs, a few jerseys, and some photos packed away. A lot of it was his dad's. This would give him a nice place to display them."

"Well," Tracy said, "you have almost four weeks till the thirtieth. You just need to find a contractor who can get it done by then."

"True. I'd love to have it be a surprise too. I don't know how I'll manage that."

Tracy tapped a finger against her chin. "Maybe the contractor can do a lot of the prep work off-site, like building the shelving and such, then install it all while Miles is at work. It's just one room in the house, so painting shouldn't take all that long."

"Or I could convince Miles that we should go on vacation once school is out, and I could arrange for the work to be done then."

"When's the last day?" Tracy asked.

"I have a countdown. I love teaching, but it's always nice to have a break, especially now that Miles and I are married. School ends on the seventeenth. That's nearly two weeks before Miles's birthday."

"So figure out somewhere you want to go and make it happen."

"Miles has been talking about taking a vacation this summer, but I'm not sure if he has a specific time in mind. If he can get another doctor to take his appointments while we're gone, I guess it could work."

"Or maybe some of them could be rescheduled," Tracy said. "Even general practitioners need some time off once in a while. Especially the newlywed ones."

"He'll probably tell me he needs more planning time, but I'll see what I can do."

"Good." Tracy rummaged in her box of photos again and pulled out one of the two of them on Halloween.

"Who was I supposed to be? A bobby-soxer?" Amy asked, peering at her seven-year-old self in a sweater and pleated skirt, with her hair in a ponytail. "And how did Mom get your hair to do that?"

Tracy chuckled. "She braided it around some strips of quilt batting and then twisted it all up into cinnamon buns, like Princess Leia. She modified an old prom dress into the gown. Sort of."

"Not bad for a sixth grader. Wait a minute. I think I saw that picture of us as angels when we were really little. Dad was carrying me."

"I remember that one," Tracy said as Amy rummaged in her box.

"I'm pretty sure it was in here." Amy frowned, distracted by something at the bottom of the box. "I thought it was nothing but pictures in here."

Tracy looked over at her. "What'd you find?"

"A book or something."

"Maybe it's an album."

Amy worked her fingers under the photos until she got ahold of whatever it was then carefully tugged it free. "It's one of those accordion folders," she said, untying the string around it. "I think these are monthly bills." She peered into one of the compartments. "Yeah, utilities, car payment, insurance. 1997."

Tracy sobered. "The year Mom and Dad died."

Amy managed a smile. "Dad was always so careful with his records. I wonder how this got into a box of pictures."

"Who knows? He and Mom had the accident, and everybody had to deal with settling their estates and making sure nothing got overlooked while planning the funeral and dealing with grief. Not to mention the shock of losing them so suddenly."

"It's been almost twenty-seven years," Amy murmured. "Sometimes that feels like forever, and sometimes it feels like yesterday. I hate how much of our lives they've missed."

"Me too. But it comforts me to know they'd be overjoyed to see how happy we are."

Amy investigated a couple of the other compartments and pulled out a folded piece of paper, frowning as she read it.

"What's that?" Tracy asked.

"It's an offer to buy a house. Dad signed it."

"What house? Dad never mentioned buying another house."

"It's in Centerville, Iowa."

"Iowa?" Tracy scooted so she could read over Amy's shoulder. "Dad loved Canton. Why would he want to move to Iowa?"

"I don't know. I've never heard of Centerville." Amy felt a sudden tightness in her heart. "But they were hit on the highway coming back from that direction. Do you think they had gone up there to see this house?"

"We never knew where they'd gone that day. At least this makes sense."

"And this offer is dated the day before the accident."

They both stared at the page for a long moment. The paper showed its age, but it was in pristine condition. Dad must have tucked it away where he'd remember where it was. Clearly it hadn't been disturbed since.

"Come on," Tracy said, standing up. "Let's see what we can find out about this place."

They went to the computer in Tracy's office and entered the house's address on a maps site. Soon they were virtually walking up to the front door of a cream-colored, two-story house.

"It's big," Amy said. "I love the wide wraparound porch and the attic gables. I wonder if there are actual rooms up there."

"It's right on a lake too," Tracy said, changing the view to show the back of the house. "There's a dock."

"Mom and Dad would have liked that. I wonder which lake that is and what the town is like."

They searched for information on Centerville, Iowa. "It used to be a coal-mining town," Amy read. "And it has the biggest town square in Iowa."

"I can't see Dad and Mom wanting to live there because of the town square."

Amy smiled. "Me neither. But I think we should find out what they did want when they went up there that day. What do you think?"

Tracy grinned. "Road trip?"

"Road trip." Amy checked the computer one more time. "Centerville's about two hours away. We could go up there and back in a day."

"What are you doing this Saturday?"

Amy raised her eyebrows. "I'm pretty sure my sister and I are driving up to Centerville, Iowa."

A Note from the Editors

We hope you enjoyed another exciting volume in the Secrets from Grandma's Attic series, published by Guideposts. For over seventy-five years, Guideposts, a nonprofit organization, has been driven by a vision of a world filled with hope. We aspire to be the voice of a trusted friend, a friend who makes you feel more hopeful and connected.

By making a purchase from Guideposts, you join our community in touching millions of lives, inspiring them to believe that all things are possible through faith, hope, and prayer. Your continued support allows us to provide uplifting resources to those in need. Whether through our communities, websites, apps, or publications, we inspire our audiences, bring them together, and comfort, uplift, entertain, and guide them. Visit us at guideposts.org to learn more.

We would love to hear from you. Write us at Guideposts, P.O. Box 5815, Harlan, Iowa 51593 or call us at (800) 932-2145. Did you love *A Thief in the Night*? Leave a review for this product on guideposts.org/shop. Your feedback helps others in our community find relevant products.

Find inspiration, find faith, find Guideposts.

Shop our best sellers and favorites at
guideposts.org/shop

Or scan the QR code to go directly to our Shop

While you are waiting for the next fascinating story in Secrets from Grandma's Attic, check out some other Guideposts mystery series!

Savannah Secrets

Welcome to Savannah, Georgia, a picture-perfect Southern city known for its manicured parks, moss-covered oaks, and antebellum architecture. Walk down one of the cobblestone streets, and you'll come upon Magnolia Investigations. It is here where two friends have joined forces to unravel some of Savannah's deepest secrets. Tag along as clues are exposed, red herrings discarded, and thrilling surprises revealed. Find inspiration in the special bond between Meredith Bellefontaine and Julia Foley. Cheer the friends on as they listen to their hearts and rely on their faith to solve each new case that comes their way.

The Hidden Gate
A Fallen Petal
Double Trouble
Whispering Bells
Where Time Stood Still
The Weight of Years

Willful Transgressions
Season's Meetings
Southern Fried Secrets
The Greatest of These
Patterns of Deception
The Waving Girl
Beneath a Dragon Moon
Garden Variety Crimes
Meant for Good
A Bone to Pick
Honeybees & Legacies
True Grits
Sapphire Secret
Jingle Bell Heist
Buried Secrets
A Puzzle of Pearls
Facing the Facts
Resurrecting Trouble
Forever and a Day

Mysteries of Martha's Vineyard

Priscilla Latham Grant has inherited a lighthouse! So with not much more than a strong will and a sore heart, the recent widow says goodbye to her lifelong Kansas home and heads to the quaint and historic island of Martha's Vineyard, Massachusetts. There, she comes face-to-face with adventures, which include her trusty canine friend, Jake, three delightful cousins she didn't know she had, and Gerald O'Bannon, a handsome Coast Guard captain—plus head-scratching mysteries that crop up with surprising regularity.

A Light in the Darkness
Like a Fish Out of Water
Adrift
Maiden of the Mist
Making Waves
Don't Rock the Boat
A Port in the Storm
Thicker Than Water
Swept Away
Bridge Over Troubled Waters
Smoke on the Water
Shifting Sands

SECRETS FROM GRANDMA'S ATTIC

Shark Bait
Seascape in Shadows
Storm Tide
Water Flows Uphill
Catch of the Day
Beyond the Sea
Wider Than an Ocean
Sheeps Passing in the Night
Sail Away Home
Waves of Doubt
Lifeline
Flotsam & Jetsam
Just Over the Horizon

Miracles & Mysteries
of Mercy Hospital

Four talented women from very different walks of life witness the miracles happening around them at Mercy Hospital and soon become fast friends. Join Joy Atkins, Evelyn Perry, Anne Mabry, and Shirley Bashore as, together, they solve the puzzling mysteries that arise at this Charleston, South Carolina, historic hospital—rumored to be under the protection of a guardian angel. Come along as our quartet of faithful friends solve mysteries, stumble upon a few of the hospital's hidden and forgotten passageways, and discover historical treasures along the way! This fast-paced series is filled with inspiration, adventure, mystery, delightful humor, and loads of Southern charm!

Where Mercy Begins
Prescription for Mystery
Angels Watching Over Me
A Change of Art
Conscious Decisions
Surrounded by Mercy
Broken Bonds
Mercy's Healing

SECRETS FROM GRANDMA'S ATTIC

To Heal a Heart
A Cross to Bear
Merciful Secrecy
Sunken Hopes
Hair Today, Gone Tomorrow
Pain Relief
Redeemed by Mercy
A Genius Solution
A Hard Pill to Swallow
Ill at Ease
'Twas the Clue Before Christmas

Find more inspiring stories in these best-loved Guideposts fiction series!

Mysteries of Lancaster County
Follow the Classen sisters as they unravel clues and uncover hidden secrets in Mysteries of Lancaster County. As you get to know these women and their friends, you'll see how God brings each of them together for a fresh start in life.

Secrets of Wayfarers Inn
Retired schoolteachers find themselves owners of an old warehouse-turned-inn that is filled with hidden passages, buried secrets, and stunning surprises that will set them on a course to puzzling mysteries from the Underground Railroad.

Tearoom Mysteries Series
Mix one stately Victorian home, a charming lakeside town in Maine, and two adventurous cousins with a passion for tea and hospitality. Add a large scoop of intriguing mystery, and sprinkle generously with faith, family, and friends, and you have the recipe for Tearoom Mysteries.

Ordinary Women of the Bible
Richly imagined stories—based on facts from the Bible—have all the plot twists and suspense of a great mystery, while bringing you fascinating insights on what it was like to be a woman living in the ancient world.

To learn more about these books, visit Guideposts.org/Shop